THE CRAFT OF FICTION

REVISED EDITION

THE CRAFT OF FICTION

REVISED EDITION

william c. knott

*state university of new york
at potsdam*

reston publishing company, inc.

*a prentice-hall company
reston, virginia*

Library of Congress Cataloging in Publication Data

Knott, William,
    The craft of fiction.

    Bibliography: p.
    Includes index.
    1. Fiction—Technique. I. Title.
PN3355.K57 1977   808.3   76-46322
ISBN 0-87909-129-0
ISBN 0-87909-131-2 pbk.

© 1977 by Reston Publishing Company, Inc.
A Prentice-Hall Company
Reston, Virginia 22090

10 9 8 7 6 5 4 3 2 1

Printed in the United States of America

This book is dedicated to Lew Turco
a fine poet and
a friend indeed

contents

preface

Because there are many varieties of books and stories on the bookshelves, any one of which you may prefer to write, it seemed wise when discussing the special techniques practiced in the creation of fiction to steer a middle course between the specific and the general, and between this and that genre. It is hoped, therefore, that what has been included in the chapters that follow will prove to be of use no matter what type of fiction you should decide to write, for those general principles covered in the text have proven basic to all good fiction writing.

THE CRAFT OF FICTION

REVISED EDITION

part one

THE WRITER AND HIS WORLD

*What follows is a brief discussion of certain attitudes and
assumptions I have found to be so misleading and
inappropriate that they seriously hinder the student
writer's chance of achieving even a modest success. The
most damaging of these attitudes and assumptions are
clustered about three basic topics: writing for money, the
fictional world as opposed to the real world, and the
degree of commitment required of the writer.
Accordingly, you might do well to read these three
chapters carefully before proceeding further into the text,
since they may well convince you of the wisdom of
retaining your present amateur status. On the other hand,
what follows could embolden you to abandon that status
and begin to think of yourself as a professional.*

1

chapter one

This Precarious Profession

"No man but a blockhead ever wrote except for money."
SAMUEL JOHNSON

*Many feel it is bad form, or worse, for a student of
writing – indeed, for any writer – to give serious
consideration to the possibility of monetary reward. Yet I
have been approached on countless occasions by
individuals who expect to realize quick fortunes on the
strength of a novel or short story they are in the process
of writing. Others, equally annoying, are openly
suspicious of me. After all, they imply, if I have
published so many books, why am I not riding around in
a Rolls Royce? Just what, then, are the financial realities
of this profession? This chapter should give you some
needed perspective on this troublesome matter.*

Writing for Money

What the good Doctor Johnson meant by that remark, of course, was that no one but a blockhead works for nothing. There comes a point in every endeavor, no matter how genuinely unselfish the motive, no matter how fulfilling the task, when *some* just compensation is not only legitimate, but downright necessary.

Writers — like lawyers, doctors, politicians, businessmen, jockeys, gangsters, used-car salesmen, composers, mechanics, artists, professors of English, editors, and plumbers — have to eat on a fairly regular basis and are responsible, in many cases, for providing clothing and shelter for their young. Unless, therefore, the writer is paid for his or her talents, that writer will have extreme difficulty functioning in this society. The writer who insists on writing without compensation will soon find himself unable to write. The reason Dr. Johnson and *all* professional writers demand payment is not that they are unregenerate hacks who have sold their talents to the highest bidder; rather, they simply enjoy writing and wish to continue to be able to work at their craft, however modest the fruits of their talents may be.

Indeed, for the average writer, far from being the great enemy to a writing career, money is the one indispensable element without which there can be no career, pious hopes to the contrary. As one who has known many professional writers personally, I can state with some authority that the well-paid writer is the happiest of mortals — and as a result, one of the most creative.

Unfortunately, few students — of whatever age — can hope for much real financial backing for their first creative efforts. Unhappily, this is often true for many established professionals as well. Schools, colleges, and newspapers, as well as the editorial staffs of magazines and publishing houses, contain many writers who are working solely to supplement their writing income.

In short, it does not always follow that wealth and fame are the certain rewards of a writing career. It is only fair to point out, in fact, one very lamentable but inescapable truth, one that the fledgling writer had better learn to live with: *Writers do not make very much money.* Not too long ago, in a survey of members of the Author's League, it was found that the average free-lance writer earns just over $3,000 a year — not a very princely sum, you must admit.

Of course some writers of fiction do make it big, and it

gives all writers heart when they see one of their number succeed. But these writers are the exceptions, not the rule.

The Shrinking Fiction Market

Twenty to twenty-five years ago the ratio of fiction to non-fiction published in our magazines was three to one. Now the situation is reversed. Fiction is no longer the staple it once was, and nonfiction has moved in to take its place. What has happened to cause this? Well, for one thing, television now provides the kind of escape fiction that used to be the chief bill of fare in the so-called pulp and mass slick publications. Another reason is that the real world has proven so complex, so fascinating, and so deadly that today the average reader turns to it as avidly as he once turned to fiction. Think over this last decade — if you had created that period as a piece of fiction, an editor might well have mailed it back to you, commenting that your writing was totally lacking in believability.

What all this implies is obvious: There are fewer markets, and there is tougher entry into those that are left. And for the very few short story markets that remain, the payment — except for *Playboy* and one or two of the top women's magazines — is disappointingly low. The confessions are having difficulty today; and even these markets seldom paid more than five cents a word — tops. *Alfred Hitchcock's Mystery Magazine,* where I placed my first mystery short story, was recently close to bankruptcy and was rescued by *Ellery Queen's Mystery Magazine,* the owner of which promptly announced his intention to keep this fine magazine alive. There are quite a few writers around who hope it can be done.

In brief, for the writer of short fiction, times are indeed rough. There was a time when a writer could earn a fine yearly income writing short stories alone. But that day is past.

What This Means to You

What is left, then, for the fiction writer are the paperback or category novel for the softcover houses and the mainstream novel for those few hardcover publishers which still accept unsolicited manuscripts — a tribe whose number grows rapidly less as publishers slash their staffs, merge, change direction, or simply disappear. (Recently, a science-fiction manu-

5

script of mine vanished without a trace when an entire editorial staff was swept out one door and a new staff ushered in the other.) I could go on, but why belabor the point?

Of course I realize how negative this must sound to you. And yet, what choice have I? This book is being written for the *serious* student of writing, not for the Sunday writer. It would not be honest for me to sugarcoat the facts.

Summary

It will take hard work and a clearly remarkable commitment for any student of writing today to master its difficulties well enough to support himself or herself in this society. At best, the young writer will have to consider some kind of paying job while he or she finishes this apprenticeship. And then the initiate will have a willful and seemingly capricious publishing world to contend with from that point on.

Of course, neither the blockhead who assumes that paid publication need not be a consideration nor the fool who assumes that certain fame and riches are waiting on his first book is typical of most students. But somewhere between those two extremes you will have to place yourself.

Hopefully, you will see yourself as squarely in the middle. You do not expect to get rich as a result of your writing; but neither will you deem it a privilege to starve. And finally, you will do what you must to learn your craft thoroughly, for you realize that this is one race that is not only to the quick, but to those who know how to endure.

And—confident in your craft—you will endure. For every day, despite the enormous odds, new writers are being discovered and their work is being published. You could be one of them.

That is my hope, as it must be yours. The odds—I repeat—are steep, but you *can* beat them.

Questions for Study and Discussion

1. When you want to read a short story today, to what periodicals do you turn? *Playboy? The New Yorker?* Or to your favorite literary magazine? Have you noticed how difficult it is today to find good short fiction?

2. To what extent has the paperback novel come to dominate your reading choices? How often do you go to the

bookstore to purchase a hardcover work of fiction? How much do you or your friends or older members of your family depend on the book clubs?

3. Would you have purchased this book or enrolled in this class if you had realized that writers were so poorly paid? Do these facts about the profession of fiction writing discourage you? Do you think writing should be a nonremunerative hobby or sideline? When writers discuss money, are you pained?

chapter two
The Nature of Fiction

"The image that fiction presents is purged of the distractions, confusions and accidents of ordinary life."
ROBERT PENN WARREN

Fiction is not reality. Unless this quite crucial distinction is made, the would-be writer will be constantly in trouble when it comes to treatment and selection of material, in short, to any useful understanding of the craft of fiction. This difference is the burden of the following chapter, and I hope that when you have finished it, you will be able to make this distinction yourself.

One of the most difficult things to teach the beginning writer is the radical difference between the world as he knows it and the world of fiction. For what happens to people in real life bears little resemblance to what happens to them in fiction. Life is not fiction, and so-called "true-to-life" fiction is not really telling it the way it is—not at all.

The Real World

This world of ours is not a stranger to mad coincidence. It is a place where people act out their little dramas with a numbing lack of intelligent purpose, where good fortune as well as bad seems to turn up with the same inexplicable lack of logic: a lucky break with a sweepstakes ticket one moment, a heart attack while watching television the next.

Furthermore, our companions on this journey are, after all is said and done, strangers to us. Can we hear what thoughts—what hopes and fears—animate their consciousness as they sit across from us at the dinner table? Perhaps we think we can; but it is a wise man who concludes that he can never presume to know what goes on in the hearts and minds of others, no matter how close they are to him, no matter how dear.

If life, for most of us then, is a series of briefly glimpsed vistas, unrealized dreams, dimly perceived people, and stories that seem to have no beginning and no end, it is definitely not this way in fiction. Here at last is a world all of a piece. The people we meet in the books we read are people we know as we have known no one else in all our lives. We are privy to their most intimate thoughts, their secret dreams, even their nightmares. Nothing is hidden from us— or so it appears. What these people do, therefore, is understandable to us. Any seeming inconsistencies in their behavior are immediately explained away by the circumstances of their lives. When they say or do something, we know why they have said or done it. If they are kind and thoughtful, they stay that way throughout the story—unless something we understand and can sympathize with happens to them, causing them to change.

For these fictional people there are no outrageous coincidences—no sudden, inexplicable disasters that wipe out their hope and their story in midstream. Whatever unexpected adventures may befall them, we are skillfully led to expect in advance. And when cruel chance is allowed to play its part in their lives, it is held in reasonable and bearable check by the writer, lest it be considered too outrageous or melodramatic to be believable.

The result is a world that comforts us with its order and people that comfort us with their consistency. Murder and mayhem, death and sorrow are not strangers to this world. On the contrary. But always the unpleasantness serves a purpose or makes a point.

But It Really Happened!

Often, when a young writer is defending a particularly gratuitous plot development to me, he will look at me pityingly and announce that it really happened that way. And he will say it in such a way as to leave no doubt that as far as he is concerned I have been found out, that all I have been telling him concerning the lack of motivation for this character's actions, the unlikelihood that such and such could occur as a result—all this was now completely and unalterably confounded by that one simple assertion.

The problem is that it makes not a particle of difference that it really happened. What matters is whether or not the reader will be able to believe, as he reads, that it really happened this way.

Recently a friend approached me with a great idea for a story. He couldn't wait to tell me all about it. Here's how it went:

> A good friend of his had divorced his first wife. He had never really been in love with her, it seemed, and had only married her on the rebound from a love affair that had gone sour. Once his marriage was dissolved, he sold all his possessions and moved to California. One day, on a shopping trip to San Francisco, he saw, walking toward him on the sidewalk . . . guess who? That's right. His old flame. She too had been married and divorced and was just as lonely for him as he was for her. At last report they were getting along splendidly, with wedding bells chiming in the wings.

Of course I had to tell my friend I couldn't use his story, since in fact, as I explained, it was not a story at all, but rather an account of an extraordinary coincidence—the kind of coincidence that is simply not allowed in fiction. And it is not allowed for a very good reason. It would not be believed. Ask yourself this: In all the novels, motion pictures, and television dramas you have read and watched in the past year or so, how many of them were resolved by a lucky coincidence? That's right. Not one.

Furthermore, the protagonist of my friend's "story" was not a very effective one at all because he had done absolutely nothing to seek out his old flame. He had simply accepted his fate, obviously did his best to forget what happened—and was then presented with this incredible stroke of luck.

"But it really happened!" my friend protested.

And there's no doubt, of course, that this remarkable coincidence did take place exactly as my friend described it. After all, such marvelous changes in fortune—for good as well as for bad—happen to those all around us and even to ourselves on occasion. Life *is* like that. But unfortunately for my friend and for any would-be authors there is considerably more to creating fiction than simply changing the names of the real people, dreaming up an appropriate title and then writing down whatever bizarre incidents one finds recounted in the *The National Enquirer.*

Can't the Writer Use Incidents From Life?

Of course the writer can, for a start. And quite often the writer does use incidents from life to get a story or novel going. But the important point to remember in this regard is that once you begin to write, you are on your own; and any attempt on your part to bend your story to make it conform to the way it "really happened" will simply ruin the whole thing, for the reality you are imposing on it from without will succeed only in stifling the natural form your story should be assuming as it grows within your imagination. For it is your imagination, you see, that must take over, that must embellish, retouch and reshape the reality you are using as a starting point.

Say, for example, you wished to use the assassination of John F. Kennedy as the basis for a novel. You will have to begin changing actuality from the start. You will have to create people who didn't exist, invent dialogue and incidents leading up to that fatal shot, imagine scenes that will establish beyond a question Oswald's marksmanship. And most important of all you will have to establish his motivation—

12

this last, something that even Oswald's wife could not seem to fathom.

As you write, you will find a form emerging from all the events, a rationale that will soon dominate and shape what you write. It is inevitable. But it will not necessarily be the way it was for Oswald or for any of the others caught up in this event with him. Nevertheless, this will have to be the way it is for you, the writer, as you fashion *your* fictional version of what happened in Dallas that afternoon.

Can the Writer Use Real People?

Again, the answer is that the writer may start with a person he or she knows, but that is not how he or she will finish. As mentioned before, we don't really *know* those people around us. Of course, we may be aware of how they walk, how they talk, and what they look like, but that is not nearly enough for fiction. As a result, we will have to create their thoughts, reconstruct their motives, invent their pasts—and all in accordance with the logic of their situation in the world we are creating for them.

Also, it must be kept in mind that people in real life make poor models for fictional characters *primarily because of the way they deal with their problems*. They act falteringly. They are not consistent. They fail to analyze carefully their situation and as a result have only the fuzziest idea of where their troubles lie. They give up for foolish reasons and go ahead when all reason would tell them to halt. In addition to all this, they harbor inconsistent prejudices and act on contradictory premises without seeing the contradictions. And all of this because they are basically unaware of most of the reasons why they do what they do.

As a result, people in real life seldom handle their problems as directly or effectively as the reader expects them to do in fiction. They seldom mount consistent attacks on their problems at all. They simply learn to live with them, try to forget them or hope to outgrow them. For the longest time many people can even convince themselves that they have no problem at all—as they talk around it, think around it, and do their best to live around it.

And of course many times things do "work themselves out." The toothache goes away. The unhappiness in a poor marriage becomes blunted as a kind of give-and-take

13

emerges. A tyrannical boss dies suddenly. Something fortuitous happens. But this is not really very dramatic. And not at all useful for the writer of fiction.

In comparison, think of Ahab's pursuit of Moby Dick, Arrowsmith challenging the deadly world of microbes, Sister Carrie learning ever so cleverly and ever so quietly how to beat the system, Lord Jim seeking to redeem himself after that one fateful moment of weakness, the hinge on which his life swung. And then there is Tolstoy's magnificent cast of characters: Pierre, Natasha, Anna Karenina, Levin, Ivan Ilych; or Dostoyevsky's tormented souls, Raskolnikov, especially.

There are more great fictional characters I could mention, of course; even as I pause in this catalogue still others crowd about me. And I am sure you have your own list. But for now those few characters are enough. The point, surely, is obvious. These are all powerful characters who do not—who cannot—lie still and wait for Providence to save them, even though this may be the only thing that can. They itch, so they scratch. They howl and act—however reluctantly, as in Hamlet's case—as they face up to and perhaps vanquish those forces arrayed against them.

Fictional characters, then, to be memorable and worth reading about—at least for this writer—must be capable of attempting some definite resolution to their problems. In addition, during this effort they should arrive at some insight into themselves and into the lives they lead. They will get a divorce, for instance, but—unlike so many of us, it seems—they will manage to learn something about themselves in the process. Furthermore, when we first meet them they are not ignoring the problem, but are rising, in some fashion at least, to the challenge fate has thrown them.

14 Even Camus' Stranger, Meursault, no matter how infuriatingly passive he may appear at first, is plainly at odds with the automaton he has become until at last he bursts out of the prison of himself, murders a man, and then while awaiting execution finds himself cleansed of hope, able finally to understand and accept the "benign indifference of the universe."

In other words, the writer who studies—as he should—other writers must look beyond the obvious. Just because an author labors long and skillfully to give the reader the impression that his novels or stories are simply carbon copies of a formless reality filled with the same passive, meaningless characters we find in life—this does not mean that what the writer has written has no form or that its characters have not been created to fit a purposeful design.

Molly Bloom's interior monologue at the close of *Ulysses*, as one example, is certainly *not* a meaningless ramble, but rather a brilliantly controlled, structured artifact contrived by James Joyce, surely one of the finest craftsmen of our time. The art is in the way Molly's thoughts *appear* to be rambling without direction or purpose when in truth we are being told precisely what Joyce wants us to know about Molly Bloom.

The great characters in fiction, then—including such seemingly atypical protagonists as Meursault and Molly Bloom—are not simply artless copies of real people. They are the conscious creations of intelligent, highly gifted craftsmen.

The Writer as Fabricator

Even if the real world cannot be used as a blueprint for your fiction, it can be a starting point. But *only* a starting point. As you look around you, begin to invent. Start asking questions. Then provide your own answers, without worrying about whether or not they are "true," for the life you witness around you must be only the starting point for that other world your imagination must build.

And what kind of world will this be? As Robert Penn Warren says, "a world purged of the distractions, confusions and accidents of ordinary life."

What this means is that your major characters will have to be provided with reasons, good reasons, for doing what they do. This is called giving them motivation. Time is compressed as much as possible, so that there does not appear to be any lag as the story or novel progresses. Only those incidents which develop the theme and advance the story will be written about in detail, as much of the minutiae of daily life is overlooked: meals, elimination, irrelevant quarrels and conversations, annoying but pointless delays, and so on. The dialogue will be to the point, developing character and helping to advance the story line. It is, in short, a streamlined world—and one designed, essentially, for the maximum dramatic impact.

Naturally, this is a deception—a lie about life—which means that the writer must be an expert prevaricator, able to create the illusion that this formalized, speeded-up universe he or she spreads before the reader is real when in fact it is only an elaborate fabrication. But this is not a simple task. Indeed, the writer who cannot convince the reader of the reality of this unreal world has failed in the writer's primary task. But it can be done. Writers are doing it every day.

How, for instance, does Franz Kafka make us believe that a man could be transformed overnight into a gigantic cockroach? By simply stating this melancholy fact in his opening sentence: *As Gregor Samsa awoke one morning from uneasy dreams he found himself transformed in his bed into a gigantic insect.* The clear statement of Kafka's premise enables Kafka to go on from that point with perfect fictional logic. And, indeed, what follows *is* perfectly logical.

And that last is an important point to remember. Unlike the illogic of much that happens to us in this real world, that fictional land we are creating — even the nightscapes of Kafka — must follow a rigidly logical cast. The most fantastic tales are but logical developments from a single basic premise stated at the outset by the author and accepted by the reader, no matter how illogical or contrary to the laws of nature this premise may be.

Once the reader accepts the fact that Gregor Samsa has been transformed overnight into a cockroach, for instance, the reader will accept as well all that which *logically* follows from that premise — and as long as Kafka develops his story from that premise and does not violate it arbitrarily, the reader will find himself within the walls of that terrible bedroom watching in horror as Gregor's little legs struggle wildly, futilely. . . .

16   In short, unlike life, little of worth happens in a story or novel by chance or arbitrary accident. Though life may be filled with marvelous coincidences and cluttered with annoying and sometimes deadly happenstances — all apparently without design — the novel or short story cannot afford that luxury. It must be compressed, ordered, and — above all — logical.

You would do well to think of fiction, then, as a story or novel created by one who has deliberately set out to construct a world and its inhabitants "purged" of the untidy, multifarious nuisances and clutter of the real world, as the writer compresses time, alters some facts and embellishes others. And this tidily compressed world in which people know where they are going and manage somehow to get there is a world demanded by the reader, who sometimes wants to be soothed, at other times enlightened, even horrified — but always to be entertained.

Of course, mention of the reader's role in all this may surprise some — and offend others. And certainly no one has ever determined scientifically just why the reader seems to need in his fiction what years of reading and writing fiction have convinced me he does. But the writer must never forget that the reader is the other half of that equation he or she is trying to solve in this text — and any contemptuous dismissal of that fact will only gain for that writer's efforts the massive indifference such arrogance deserves.

To summarize: Fiction is a fabrication — not a mirror of reality — and this fabrication is designed to delight or at least catch the attention of the reader. It would seem to be a wise course, therefore, to keep this difference between fiction and reality in mind as you work through this text. Otherwise, you will find yourself in constant difficulty, not only in selecting subjects for your fiction, but in choosing and delineating characters, and finally in resolving those situations your fiction is exploring.

Questions for Study and Discussion

1. How many times have you tried to capture in fiction what you know "really happened?" What were the results?

2. Do you know what your fellow students are thinking as they sit beside you? How do you *really* feel about your spouse? Do you think you know how your spouse feels about you?

3. How much do you know about your own motives? Or those of your friends and relatives? Can you articulate clearly your present goals, likes, dislikes, problems? How are you going to go about solving the most pressing problems you now face?

4. What have you really learned from what has happened so far in your life? How many people do you know who actually keep repeating their mistakes? List a few. Discuss them.

5. A few famous fictional characters and their authors were mentioned in this chapter. If this suggests you should look them up, you would not be far wrong. Indeed, how

much *do* you read? Why not make a list of your own favorite fictional characters? It will tell you much about yourself and what direction you should take as a writer.

Suggestions for Writing

1. Select a news item that interests you and use it as the basis for a short story or fictional incident in a longer work, noting as you work how much has to be invented in order for you to make your fictional re-creation logical as well as believable.

2. Retell as fiction an incident in which you and someone close to you took part. When you finish, read the account to that other person and note how your account changes "what really happened."

3. Keep a minute-by-minute account of a typical morning, afternoon, or evening. Then rewrite this same time span as fiction, noting how much you have to edit in order to rid your account of the miring minutiae of nonfictional reality.

chapter three

Are You a Writer?

Interviewer: *"What determined you to become a writer?"*
Frank O'Connor: *"I've never been anything else."*

*The writer's joy is to write. It is also his compulsion, a
monomania that one should not lightly assume. Indeed,
if by now you are beginning to have some doubts about
the blessings of a writing career, you had best read on.
This chapter may possibly settle the matter for you once
and for all. But if your need to write is already firmly
established, you may find that out as well.*

When people approach me after a talk or at the conclusion of a writing class and tell me that they want to become professional writers, I am always saddened at first and just a little concerned for them. Do they realize, I wonder, what they are letting themselves in for?

I have witnessed two appalling tragedies, resulting almost entirely from ignorance concerning the facts of a writing career. Two middle-aged men suddenly abandoned their jobs—in one case, a fellow sold a thriving business—in order to pursue careers in the writing of fiction. What was tragic was that neither of these people seemed to have the slightest idea of the enormous amount of time it takes to become a successful writer of fiction today.

The result, in both cases, was that the families were torn apart—and divorce with its accompanying heartache followed. I am convinced that if these two individuals had been given a more realistic understanding of how awesomely difficult it is to pursue a successful writing career, these tragedies need not have occurred. In other words, someone should have made them understand that a career in writing, like any other career, demands at the very least a long and difficult apprenticeship before any real success can be expected.

I hope that these opening chapters will help you, the student writer, to understand this truth.

Sitting and Bleeding

Writing is a pleasure, of course. At the inception of each novel or story, the first flash of the work in its entirety gives the writer a wonderful exhilaration. And it is in that burst of enthusiasm and hope that the writer sets to work. But from then on, that is precisely what it is: work. And somehow, through the grueling days and weeks and months, the writer must hold to that original conception. And it is the dim memory of that first idea which does carry the writer through—that and the occasional bursts of good writing and the pleasure of watching the people in his or her story spring to life. Finally, when the writer has finished and knows that every effort has been bent to the realization of that original ideal, the writer may be said to be truly happy.

But the distance between those two moments is great and makes for a painful trek indeed. As Hemingway is reported to have said, "It is easy to write. Just sit in front of your typewriter and bleed."

Indeed, as soon as student writers and acquaintances of mine begin to grasp this potent fact, they come to me with anxious questions, all phrased differently, but each one asking basically the same thing:

> *"I just want to know if it makes any sense for me to go on."*
>
> *"I've been working on it for years and my husband thinks it's great. But I don't know. Would you look at it?"*
>
> *"Am I just wasting my time?"*
>
> *"All I want you to tell me is if this shows talent. Would you tell me if it does?"*

And each time I am asked to make this judgment, I refuse. If I told a student that his or her work was utterly lacking in talent, I might be right—but what I said would also be totally irrelevant. For I have seen students with great talent who never seem able to direct it or to make anything productive grow from it.

Naturally, the human thing is to want to reassure these people, to encourage them to go on with their work. For one thing, I know how it fills their hours, how it stimulates them to life and makes them aware of the people around them. I do not want them to lose that. Nevertheless, I hold back telling them anything one way or the other and try to get them to consider a few questions, the answers to which may help them settle their doubts for themselves.

Perhaps now is the time for you to try answering these questions as well.

Do You Need to Write?

By need I mean the constant, nagging urge to get off somewhere by yourself with a pen and paper and start putting down what you feel. It should be a habit—almost a bad habit, like chain-smoking. Indeed, most of the writers I know are somewhat compulsive human beings. As a result, they are often disappointingly boring. They don't want to talk, they want to write; they don't want to play games, they want to write; they don't want to visit, they want to write.

They don't want to do much of anything, in fact—unless it can be related in some way to that story or novel they are currently in the process of writing. Now ask yourself: How much like this are you?

How Long Have You Been Writing?

Recall Frank O'Connor's remark quoted at the beginning of this chapter. In effect, he was saying that he had never been anything else but a writer. That means, of course, that as long as he could remember he was either planning to write or writing. What about you? Is that the way it was with you? Were you always scribbling something? Did reading an exciting story or novel make you want to write one as good— or better?

If not, examine your motives now. Why this sudden urge to write? Is it that you've heard about all the money so and so made on his latest best seller, and having read the book yourself, you have concluded you could easily do as well? All you need now is someone to type up what you've written after you've got it all down. You don't have time for writing at the moment, but you'll get to it next summer, when you'll have more time.

And of course you're looking forward to the prestige and fame that comes with being a famous writer. You're already going around letting people know in a casual way that you write, that you've got this great idea for a novel. In your fantasies you're now beginning to see yourself on one of those talk shows, perhaps sharing the spotlight with Truman Capote.

I've drawn this portrait with pretty broad brush strokes, but despite the exaggeration, this *is* the kind of mentality writers are always meeting at parties, at conferences, at bars.

If these *are* your reasons for wanting to write, think again.

How Much of a Commitment is Required?

The answer is that you must make the kind of commitment that will effectively subordinate almost every effort and interest to the mastering of the craft.

For this reason it is best if you remain single for a while. Of course, you will probably—like most of us—find this advice somewhat difficult to follow. If you do marry, then, surely it would be only good sense for you to discuss seriously with your potential partner the ramifications of your decision to be a writer — especially the fact that you may prefer to set weekends and holidays aside for the typewriter. At the very least, your spouse should be warned of your need to write — and convinced of it, as well.

Otherwise, there might be trouble. I remember once when a woman in one of my writing classes confessed after class one night that the reason she did not have anything for discussion that evening was that her husband had stormed into her sewing room while she was typing and hurled the huge Remington typewriter to the floor, breaking it. She finished her book, I might add — but her experience offers an example of what can happen.

Furthermore, unless you are a rarity, you will — at least at first — be unable to support yourself on the money you make as a writer. You will have to take some job in order to earn money; and as a result, writing will become a part-time avocation — something you will have to squeeze in when all those about you may be having a good time, and wanting you to join in.

Again, this will make you a pest to those who know you — and to those with whom you live. All this effort, all this time away from normal people and normal activities — and what, everyone will ask, have you to show for it? Piles of returned manuscripts, that's all. Everyone will wonder if it's all worth it. And so will you — at times.

But you keep on writing. *That's* commitment. Do you think you are capable of that kind of effort?

23

Do You Know Enough to Write?

It is strange how few young writers realize that they must know something about the world around them in order to write about that world. When you write, you write about people and their society. How much, then, do you know — really know — about psychology? How much do you know about the world around you?

As a writer you will be called upon to know all kinds of simple but important facts. Exact nomenclature for all sorts of odd items will have to be at your fingertips, since you've simply got to know what to call things. Physiology, mechanics, astronomy, biology, the finer points of technology, the internal combustion engine, electricity, history, geography—the list is practically endless.

You must read voraciously in all fields and listen carefully to specialists when they discourse about their specialty—from dentists to bartenders. Think of what you should know about the criminal mind, criminal law, penology, police procedure, the law, penal institutions, and so on just to write a detective story—one that may not even be reviewed as a serious novel. I am not saying that you cannot write a mystery novel without such specialized knowledge; but I will simply remind you that the man who created Perry Mason was a fine criminal lawyer.

Of course, much of this knowledge gap can be filled with research. But you'll find that if you continue to study and read broadly on your own without regard to a specific story or novel, you will be building an inventory from which crucial facts, ideas, and solutions will spring when—much later, mulling over a story line or a character—you will most need the information.

How do you measure up? Just how close are you to matching this portrait of the curious writer? What do you really *know* about this world? If you're not a voracious reader, if you're not constantly asking questions and listening to the answers, if you're not *aware* of how little you know, do you really think you will be able to write authoritatively about the people and events around you?

Do You Have Talent?

24 And now for the big question. Everything has led up to this. After all, you ask, why break your neck for a lifetime if you do not have the talent to make anything of all that need, all that commitment? It's a good question.

Unfortunately, the answer, I feel, will only disappoint you. It is this: You can answer that question by not bothering to ask it, by just continuing to write, no matter what.

Besides, does it really matter? If you're a writer, you'll write anyway. Nothing will be able to stop that. If you don't have enough talent to match the desire, you'll simply not publish much or often. You may not even publish at all. Yet this fact will not matter, should not matter, as you continue to write year after year. I've known people who have written diligently most of their lives without publishing a word. It appears that they just didn't have enough talent, after all. But, as I said before, that fact was irrelevant.

In short, for all practical purposes, the desire to write is all the talent you need.

To sum up this first part, I hope that now you have a realistic appreciation of the difficulties involved in writing fiction and of the fact that this is not the quickest way to get rich, especially since the market for fiction continues to shrink. Fiction itself is a complex construction, not a simple, easy-to-master copy of life; and knowing this difference will aid you in your soon-to-begin search for characters and their stories. Finally, no one can tell you if you should make the kind of total commitment required or if you have the talent it takes to succeed in this demanding profession. These are questions you will have to answer for yourself.

Accordingly, you now know what you are in for, and what fiction really is—and you are closer to some understanding of your suitability for the writing profession. Now you are ready to go on to a study of the nuts and bolts of writing fiction.

Questions for Study and Discussion

1. When did you first begin to write? Why did you write? Was it to win a prize, to make money? Discuss your motives honestly. All you have to lose are your pretensions.

2. Do you plan to get married and still become a writer? If you are already married, does your spouse understand how important your commitment to writing is? Have you made this clear? If not, why not?

3. What do you read beside other novelists or short story writers? How wide is your fund of knowledge? Do you consider yourself an expert in any skill or vocation other than that of a student? What do you know about psychology, for instance?

Suggestions for Writing

1. Write a short biography of yourself up to this point, highlighting your development as a writer.

2. Write a short biographical account of any writer's early years of struggle, when he or she was in the process of

learning how to write for publication. Such writers as Robert Frost, Joyce Cary, Henry Miller, Jack London, Theodore Dreiser, William Faulkner, Sherwood Anderson, Anthony Burgess, Kurt Vonnegut should provide you with plenty of excruciating examples.

3. Interview any local writer of fiction. Discuss the impact of his or her vocation on other members of the family. Be sure to include in the discussion the years of struggle that preceded successful publication.

part two

NUTS AND BOLTS

Now that the preliminaries are over, let's get on with the job of learning what I feel are the strictly mechanical aspects of writing fiction — the delight of any craftsman — and what I prefer to call the Nuts and Bolts of writing. It is during this portion of the text that you should begin to prepare specific fictional material which you will then be able to incorporate into a short story or novel as you work on the final chapters of the text.

chapter four

Character vs. Plot

"It begins with a character, usually, and once he stands up on his feet and begins to move, all I can do is trot along behind him with a paper and pencil trying to keep up long enough to put down what he says and does."
WILLIAM FAULKNER

"I never started from ideas but always from character."
IVAN TURGENEV

No one would say that plot is dead. But it is no longer as important as it once was. Now we look to character to help us develop our plots. After all, the writer and the reader are primarily interested in people. We need only mention the name of Anton Chekhov to realize how long this has been true. So that's where we'll start — with people.

When Plot was King

It used to be that whenever two writers got together, they would immediately begin to argue about which was more important, plot or character. This, of course, was in the days of the mass-circulation magazines, when the racks of drugstores and newsstands throughout the country were groaning under the weight of 20 to 30 different pulp and slick paper magazines, each one bulging with short stories and novelettes, with a condensed novel thrown in here and there for good measure. I remember the titles even now: *Dime Western*, *The Shadow*, *Black Mask Detective*, *Doc Savage*, *Blue Book*, *Colliers*, *Liberty*, *The Saturday Evening Post*, and many, many others.

The pulp stories and many of those published in the slick paper magazines for the most part emphasized action, swift pace, and melodrama rather than characterization in depth. The people in pulp fiction especially were simply hackneyed stereotypes; well-rounded characters seldom if ever found a place in those stories. They would have slowed the pace. Under these conditions there was really no contest: Plot was supreme. In those days all kinds of plotting devices were advertised in writer's magazines, and indeed today George Polti is still selling his thirty-six basic plot situations.

But the pulps are gone now — and with their demise, the market for mass melodrama has shifted almost entirely to the TV screen and the cheaper paperbacks. Plotting devices are of little help today. In fact, I strongly suspect that the average reader is becoming plot-weary, as a result, not of his reading habits, but of the television dramas that crowd the channels, dramas in which plot is almost all incident and in which characters are basically interchangeable stereotypes despite all the grotesqueries grafted onto them to make them seem otherwise.

People in Trouble

The formula plot tended to bend the character to fit the situation; what we have now is a story line that comes from the characters, the people in the story, which now bends to suit them. What the writer does is put an interesting person in great difficulty and go on from there, for he knows that you don't have a story unless you have some interesting person in trouble. The more interesting the person is, and the more deadly the problem, the greater will be the excitement generated by the story.

Think back to any story you have read recently. What comes to mind? All the intricacies of the plot, or the persons involved? It was the people that mattered, wasn't it? You cared about what happened to them. And that was why you read on.

Of course, we are still concerned with plot. But let us define plot as someone in trouble and go on from there. I repeat, people in trouble. We're perverse creatures, it seems. We gain little pleasure in reading about people who are *not* in some kind of a scrape. For no matter how interesting the characters you create are, they won't work for you as plotting aids unless you give each of them a *difficult* problem to solve.

This is very important. Whether or not to purchase a new car instead of a new washing machine is not much of a problem at all. Life is a problem — how it is to be lived. Marriage or divorce is a problem. Death, violent or otherwise, is a problem. A chronic illness, blindness, alcoholism, addiction, madness. *These* are problems.

Think in such terms when you create your characters. Give them hopes and fears. Find out what makes them laugh or cry — or run for cover. What do they *want?* What do they *need?*

Why does Amos Bruder's face grow ashen when he sees Tom Summers drive by in his black Buick? And what is it that keeps Mary Stowell up in her single room over the barbershop, her pale face barely visible behind the lace curtain as she looks out day after day? What is she waiting for? Whom does she hope to see?

31

Your Stable of Characters

At this point consider creating a stable of characters from which you can populate your stories and build your plots. Look around. Select any interesting characters you may know, such as the Amos Bruder or Mary Stowell I mentioned above. The oddballs, the eccentrics, the recluses. Now get a journal or a notebook, something you can carry around with you, and start describing their physical appearance first; then begin to give these people a past.

Here's where you will have to abandon reality as you begin to rely on yourself, constructing their past out of your own. As you write, your imagination will soon create backgrounds for these people that are different from your own and yet are always informed, however subtly, by your own personal remembrance of things past.

You will incorporate into their histories images and impressions you experienced in your own lifetime: how it once felt to walk on a sandy beach in bare feet, the sadness that fell unaccountably over you while walking home from school one chill autumn day, the excitement and trepidation you felt when you pushed yourself out onto the ice wearing your first pair of skates. Impressions as varied as these will become the raw material from which you will construct the history and the character of the people you are going to use in your fiction.

Here's how a typical entry in this notebook of yours might go:

> JASON RICHARDSON Tall, broad-shouldered, walks with a belligerent thrust, wears thick glasses, one lens of which — the left one — has a black patch fastened to the inside. This is to cover his blind eye, about which he is sensitive. Has a large shock of dark hair. A husky voice. When he smiles, he cocks his head just a little and lifts his face as if to say, Are you really laughing with me?
>
> He is twenty-eight years old and works as a telephone lineman. He is married to Ellen, a short, blonde, very vivacious girl he met in high school and who seems to know exactly how to handle him. She gentles him with a quick look usually, or by going over to him and placing a hand on his. His anger seems to drain almost at once.
>
> They have no children and he is sensitive about this. Ellen does not joke about it. And no one who knows Jason does either. In fact, those in the neighborhood and his fellow linemen who have children avoid the topic whenever they are with the Richardsons.
>
> When Jason was a small boy — around eight years old — he witnessed a murder, though at the time he was too young to realize what it was he was watching. He

was lying in the grass alongside the railroad tracks in the switching yard. It was toward evening, and he was hiding from Herbie, a friend of his, with whom he was playing scatter, a variant of hide-and-seek.

Two men got out of a car near the tracks, took a third one out, and half carried, half dragged him across the field and out onto the tracks. Jason thought the man being helped was drunk. He kept very still as the three men passed within a few feet of where he was hiding. They did not notice him. Jason caught the strong whiff of alcohol as they passed.

Far out in the confusing network of tracks, they let him down, then hurried back to their car, again narrowly missing Jason. As soon as they drove off, Jason got to his feet and tried to see where they had left the third man. But Jason could see nothing. Then he heard Herbie's voice and darted back across the field and beyond the road to gain another hiding place.

It was not until years later that he realized that he had witnessed the execution of the old man who ran the cigar store on Market Street. The old man had been found the next morning after a train had passed over his body sometime in the night. A shattered whiskey bottle had pointed to the obvious conclusion. The man had been suspected of child molesting, and after his death the incidence of such crimes in the neighborhood had ceased entirely.

Jason would often look closely at older members of the community to see if he could recognize the men who took part in the store owner's execution.

The first girl he had was Susan Carlson, the girl who lived on Canal Street. The first time he noticed her, she wore a purple skirt and a tight white blouse on a bright day in May. He had found himself walking home from the junior high with her that day, and soon—a wildness in both of them—they were racing across the fields in back of the car barn. It was all so quick, so heady, that later he had difficulty putting it all together in his mind. The elation he had felt afterward was like wine. He had gone around for weeks after with a kind of drunken assurance.

For a month he and Susan had met secretly whenever they could. And then, abruptly, she had disappeared with her family as the whole passel had left town in a beat-up pickup truck. He had not even been able to say goodbye to her.

Now—so many years later—he still sees her occasionally in his dreams. Sometimes she is just as she was then; at other times she is older—about the same age as Ellen. But he moves toward her and feels her against him as he did then. . . .

And so on. The character sketch can go on for pages, and will. In the above example, for instance, we have yet to get to Jason's present situation, his desires, his daily frustrations. More important, we have yet to isolate the big problem, the one that will have enough weight to get his story under way.

Soon you will feel that you know these people in your notebook as you have known few others in your life. You will add to each sketch constantly. Each person will grow more and more solid with every new entry and will then begin nudging at your subconscious, eager to get out of your notebook and into the world of fiction you should soon be able to create for them.

An excellent way to get names and streets for your characters is to get old telephone directories for names and service station maps that have blowups of small cities. Then you can place your characters accurately in your own mythical town.

One more thing. You will need help, if you are a male, in creating female characters, and if you are a female, in creating male characters. I don't know where you are going to get this help. Few male writers seem able to create truly believable female protagonists, and female writers seem to have the same difficulty with male characters. I said few. Certainly there are writers whose works provide vivid exceptions to this general rule: Flaubert's *Madame Bovary* is perhaps the outstanding example. But on the whole the statement is valid: If you are a male, it is going to be a lot easier for you to create a male than a female character. Remember this particularly when you select your lead characters.

Conflict

People, then, are your plots. But only if you know a great deal about them and only if you present them with problems they will have great difficulty in solving. As you take them through their struggle, you will generate conflict. And this element is what you *must* have, for without conflict, your story or novel will simply not have the excitement it needs to produce continuing interest in the reader. The most elaborate plot in the world is useless without the tension and excitement that conflict imparts to it.

Conflict is not something the writer can inject into the story whenever he or she feels things are getting dull. In other words, it is too late to consider the need for conflict after you have set your characters on stage. Conflict must be built into your characters and their situation from the outset. Ideally, if you build well to begin with, you can let the conflict take care of itself naturally while you concentrate on telling the story of your people.

The point is that conflict must be an outgrowth of your character's problem. It works this way: The character's effort to resolve his or her difficulties is challenged, either by other characters or by some natural element, such as the sea, the jungle, the cold, or the desert. Simply stated, the more menacing the challenge the protagonist has to contend with, the more intense the conflict. Of course it is always best if the protagonist's problems are intensified by discordant elements within the character himself: incipient madness, compulsion, alcoholism, drug addiction, phobia, prejudice—in short, anything that makes it difficult for the protagonist to succeed.

I remember a short story about a race driver I read years ago: The protagonist-driver had to win a race in a driving rainstorm with a bald tire getting balder while he fought a long suppressed fear of racing brought to the surface by the sight of a friend's accident. If that situation seems like a cliche now, it nevertheless kept me turning the pages as the tension mounted.

Of course your hero could be a bland superman type who has no inner doubts or inconsistencies, no nagging sense of loss or guilt, nothing at all to mar the clear surface of his disposition. The conflict in his case, therefore, will stem from external elements only. He has merely to catch the murderer or make sure the cattle get through Indian country safely, and the difficulties generated as he fights whatever villain or natural forces he finds arrayed against him will provide the necessary conflict.

As you can see, when we build stories with this kind of

hero, we are constructing category fiction: mysteries, spy novels fashioned in the James Bond image, science fiction, gothic or nurse novels, the kind of stories in which what is wanted are heroes or heroines larger than life, the kind that not very sophisticated readers find pleasure in identifying with — and no harm done.

Still, you will want a more interesting character. To achieve this, you combine external with internal conflict, creating thereby a much more complex lead character, one far more interesting to read about, and a hell of a lot more exciting to create: all of which means your characters should be human beings carrying about with them the same personal problems that bedevil the rest of us. And then, suddenly, they must be confronted with challenges that must be genuine, that truly threaten — that can kill perhaps, or at least alter their lives to such an extent that they will never be the same people they were before this all began.

Then we will have a story that cannot fail to generate conflict.

Solution: The Cavalry Arrives

You will probably have little difficulty presenting your main character with a life or death situation; but you'll find yourself in real creative trouble when the time comes for the solution. Here is where most beginners falter. They cop out. The horrendous challenges turn out to be paper tigers, no real problem at all. You know what I mean. It all turns out to have been a dream, or the man's wife is not really having an affair; she is just trying to convince the interior decorator to lower his fee for redesigning her husband's den. And so on.

Don't get caught trying this sort of thing.

Generally, the plot outline for most fiction goes something like this: The protagonist is presented with a problem and immediately attempts to solve it. He struggles long and hard, but internal and external forces prevent him from achieving a solution. Worse, each attempt to get himself out of his difficulty only seems to get him in deeper and deeper, until at last he finds himself at the breaking point. This is the *climax*, the moment when the struggle can go either way.

Now, how does your hero solve his dilemma?

You don't want all of this to turn out to be just a dream,

do you? And you can't have the police just happen to notice a suspicious light and come to investigate; nor can you fix it so that your hero stumbles over a paper bag containing the missing bomb sight. Since you have worked hard to make the problem a truly difficult one, the solution should be equal to it.

At this stage, look to your hero. You should know him well enough by this time so that you can — in effect — let *him* find the solution, as strange as this may sound. Only in this way will the solution be logical, the result of *his* actions, not some transparent gimmick tacked on to wrap things up nicely.

What I am suggesting is that throughout your plotting, and throughout your creation of the incidents and complications, you were following in the footsteps of your character. You had invested him with loves, hates, enthusiasms. You had created him so well, in fact, that soon *he* was taking the reins occasionally, moving sometimes in directions that surprised even you. That is why now he is ready to step in and give you the solution.

There will be times, of course, when he will offer no solution. He will simply admit his defeat and vow to go on somehow, like Oedipus — blinded but undefeated. But that too is a resolution — as long as it stems from the character himself, from *his* awareness of his situation.

Nothing brought in at the last minute, then. No wild coincidences. No sudden lucky break. Unlike life — where anything can happen and usually does — this is fiction, where such solutions are simply not allowed.

Aside from this, there are no pat answers for handling the solutions to your stories and novels. In most cases, the resolution is already in the story itself, inherent in everything the hero has said and done — if only you can allow him the liberty to find it. It is the logical outcome of all that he has experienced up to this point — and once he points out the solution, it will seem to you that it had been sitting there on your typewriter all this time, waiting most patiently for you to acknowledge its presence.

Let's Build a Plot

Between the problem and the solution is a long, long haul for you, the writer. It is the main body of your story — the meat, filled with incident, menace, and fascinating characters. At least you hope so. For one thing, as emphasized ear-

37

lier, the story line must contain conflict in order to maintain interest. And in order to do this, each scene or chapter should have its own problem to be resolved, giving us a series of mini-problems to be resolved along with the major one and thus assuring us that the level of conflict will always remain high.

Here's how it works:

The male protagonist is an addict. His wife, who has been made an addict by her husband, has decided she wants a divorce. She has just returned from the hospital where she lost her unborn child due to her drug-induced malnutrition. She wants to kick the habit to save herself and her four-year-old son. Thus our protagonist is presented with his major problem: how to save his marriage.

The addict—let's call him Fred—loves his wife and child. Accordingly, he swears he will quit the habit if his wife will only stay with him. The two argue bitterly. In a dramatic gesture, Fred throws his packet of heroin into the toilet and flushes it. But his wife—Alice—remains unconvinced of his sincerity.

End of first chapter or scene.

Fred now seeks to convince Alice of his sincerity by leaving the flat to enroll as an addict at the local hospital and seek therapy. But because of all kinds of red tape, he does not get admitted to their program that day. When he arrives home, he finds that Alice has left him, taking their son. He rushes out, frantic for a fix.

End of second major complication. In a novel, this might be the end of the second chapter.

The next scene opens with Fred getting a fix, but not before he has agreed to participate in a burglary with his fellow addict. The two plan the burglary very carefully. At last they enter the building, commit the robbery, and are on their way from the building when they are apprehended by the police and taken into custody.

End of third major complication.

Wife visits him in jail, manages to get him bailed out. He is clean, he tells her. Please help him. Alice finally agrees. Later, his friend comes to his flat with a full load of heroin, asking for permission to sleep there since he is fleeing the pusher from whom he stole the stuff. Alice says no, but Fred insists. An argument ensues. A violent one. She is forced to give in.

Fred wakes up at midnight. Alice is in the bathroom giving herself a fix. The two men join her. It is morning when the three of them come out of their stupor. The door is open, and their little boy is gone.

It is not difficult to imagine what might happen next. If anything hurts the boy, Alice will certainly turn on her husband with a vengeance. Even if the boy is found to be safe, she will nevertheless be brought face to face with the fact that as long as she stays with Fred, he is a danger both to her and her child. And Fred sees this as well, as he desperately tries to straighten himself out.

In addition, then, to the main problem, we have all these other problems generating conflict: bringing up a four-year-old under these circumstances, stealing to maintain the habit, the trial and perhaps imprisonment, the wife continually unwinding, the quarrels. . . .

Notice how in each scene or chapter a little drama is resolved. In the first Alice and Fred are quarreling, with Alice refusing to be convinced that she should stay on. In the second scene there is tension built around the question of whether or not Fred will get admitted to the hospital. Then comes the disappointment when he doesn't and the final straw when he comes home to find his wife gone. And so on.

Notice how conflict is engendered with each new complication that arises from Fred's desperate effort to keep his wife and child. And notice how relentlessly the protagonist's difficulties multiply with each new crisis, leaving him always in greater trouble than before.

Plot can be defined as a series of connected incidents— all filled with tension and conflict—that describes the path your lead character takes in his search for a way out of his difficulties. *How* he reacts, *how* he fights, *how* he grows or wilts in the course of that struggle is what your story is all about and *must* be determined by his character—something the writer has to be familiar with in order to proceed.

If you have created this character well, he will be the one who indicates at last which way to go, which solution or resolution is best; and you will be wise to follow his lead.

For this, after all, will now be *his* story.

Questions for Study and Discussion

1. Can you think of any stories or novels where the plot was not simply an account of the hero or heroine's attempt to extricate himself from some sort of dilemma? Discuss

Chekhov's stories in this light. Is there *really* no conflict, no resolution in these tales?

2. When you think of *A Christmas Carol*, what is it that you remember first—the plot or the character of Scrooge? How many stories have you read since in which the hero comes to realize that his life is predicated on false values and that to save his soul, he must reform? Yet how many of them left the impression that old Scrooge did?

3. Discuss the various plot situations you have read, or seen recently on TV or at the movies. Did you notice how easily they could be classified in terms of general story type: the chase, murder-detection-solution, the triangle, young love, the search, the survival story, and so on? In each case how did the characterization and the way this script treated these basic situations make them seem brand new?

Suggestions For Creating Your Own Characters

1. Purchase a loose-leaf notebook and do as this chapter suggests: Compile a series of character sketches. Start each new character from those around you if you wish. Go on from there. Give each person appropriate names and a history as well as traits, wishes, fears, resentments, and enthusiasms. As each new character develops, you may wish to invent scenes from his past, depicting incidents that have helped make him what he is now. The dividers in the notebook could contain the names of each one of your characters, and any new material you generate for these characters could be simply snapped into the proper section.

2. When you have created a few characters, select the one that interests you the most and build a plot based on his characteristics. Put him in trouble and describe what happens to him as he struggles to resolve his difficulties. Remember that not all stories end happily for the hero. But all of them should have a resolution. What you will be writing is a rough plot *treatment*, not the story or novel itself, a distinction that will become important later when we discuss treatment.

3. It would be helpful if you could bring in these character sketches and the plot you generate from them to the

class, where you could read them aloud and discuss them. It would help also if your fellow students or the instructor could look for any inconsistencies on the part of your character as he works his way through the plot you have constructed from him.

Then put the treatment aside for a while as you proceed to the next chapter.

chapter five

Characterization

"Characterization is an accident that flows out of action and dialogue."

JACK WOODFORD

All right. We build our stories with people. We are obliged, then, to make them live for the reader. But how is this accomplished? How does the magic of another's personality shine from your pages? You know what your people are like. But how do you get the reader to know as well? Perhaps this chapter can show you how.

Putting Your People On Stage

Placing the characters you have imagined on stage and giving them a life of their own in the world of your fancy are the beginnings of that agonizing process called writing. Up until now it has all been preparation. If you've written down any vital statistics concerning your people—and this *is* almost indispensable—what comes now is something entirely different.

Show Not Tell

In a story or novel you show your reader, you don't tell him about your people. This is what is meant by dramatizing. It does not mean employing lots of lovely descriptive adjectives and adverbs. Exposition is telling about something. Writing dramatically is showing it. It is the difference between reading a newspaper account of an automobile accident and being in the accident yourself.

What do I mean? Watch.

TELLING

Mary Lou was so kind, so sweet as she told him it was all over between them that his loss seemed doubly insupportable.

SHOWING

Mary Lou's face was a pale oval in the moonlight, her eyes luminous with concern. She leaned close and kissed him lightly on the cheek.

"I *am* sorry," she said. "So very sorry."

She took the carnation from the corsage he had given her and deftly threaded its stem through the buttonhole in his lapel. She smoothed it down gently, then looked back up into his face.

"It's not your fault, Jerry. It's nobody's fault, really. You understand that, don't you?"

He nodded. "Yes," he managed. "Of course."

"And we'll always be friends."

He started to say something—something ironic, bitter; but she placed her hand softly over his mouth.

"It's true, Jerry," she whispered. "We'll always be friends. Let's have that, at least."

She pulled her hand away from his mouth, kissed him lightly on the lips, and then was gone—a pale cloud vanishing among the willows.

TELLING

Little Marty acted like a real brat the next morning and made an awful mess on the kitchen floor, which his mother had to clean up.

SHOWING

"I don't want any," Marty said, glowering.

Marty looked as if he had not gotten enough sleep the night before. Yet Elvira knew he'd slept like a railroad tie.

"Now, Marty," Elvira said, "be a good boy and try it."

"I hate that stuff."

"Please, dear," she said. "Mustn't say hate. Try it first, then see. Oatmeal is good for you. You'll love it."

But the heartier she sounded, the darker became Marty's scowl. "I hate it," he repeated.

She sighed and placed the bowl of steaming oatmeal down in front of him. "Wait until it cools, dear," she said.

She stepped back—which was a good thing.

With one swift accurate sweep of his right arm, Marty caught the bowl perfectly and sent it spinning through the air. When it struck the floor, it did not break. Still spinning, it spewed its contents over the newly waxed floor until it came to a halt against the wall. That was when it broke.

Rushing over in an attempt to catch the spinning dish before it struck the wall, Elvira stepped into the steaming porridge. It was not secure footing. Her feet flew out from under her, and she sat down in it—heavily.

"Oh, Marty!" she moaned.

TELLING

He met her for the first time that day and was astonished at her beauty.

Leaning on the fence, he watched her move toward him, entranced with the smoothness, the easy grace of her slim figure. Just before she reached the fence, she released the reins and sent the horse toward the barn with a gentle pat on its rump.

Then she came directly toward him. He saw frank blue eyes, a fine brow with delicately molded eyebrows—natural, not painted on—the gentle oval of her face accentuated by the smooth, straw-colored hair she had tied back in a neat bun. Her nose was not quite cute or perky but straight, uncompromising—not at all unpleasant. And then she smiled, lighting her whole face.

The Difference Between Dramatizing Your Story and Writing a Treatment of It

Obviously, there is a considerable gain in immediacy and interest when the writer dramatizes in this fashion.

In fact, if the writer does not dramatize, he will in essence be writing, not a story, but a treatment—that is, a broad, general account of what happens in his story or novel, a kind of rough outline.

I once knew a fellow who wore out typewriters and filled footlockers with historical novels—massive tomes, each one. He was a history teacher and did not spare himself when it came to researching his books. The cast of characters invariably rivaled that of *War and Peace*. But this is how he wrote:

> When Captain Henshaw went to the river that morning, he met his old friend, Chief Black Hawk, and the two of them came to a quick agreement about the placement of that night's encampment. The discussion was friendly, but Henshaw noticed how restless Black Hawk's braves acted and suspected that something was not quite right. He bid goodbye to the chief in as friendly a manner as possible and hurried back to his men, anxious to find Muldoon, since there was a good chance that Muldoon might have noticed something suspicious during his last trapping expedition north of the pine country.
>
> He found Muldoon talking with some of the fur

traders from the Huron country and asked him if he'd noticed anything unusual. Muldoon considered carefully before replying, then admitted that he had noticed . . .

Difficult as this may be to believe, this sort of thing went on for page after page, chapter after chapter, book after book. The fellow's expenditure of energy was prodigious as he turned out these massive treatments of historical subjects.

The pity is that there was so much potential in all of this material. Much was happening to the characters — but the reader glimpsed it from such a distance that it was as if none of the people in these novels ever really spoke or felt a thing. They seemed to hear no war cries, to feel none of the terror they should have felt as they crumpled under the Indians' hatchets while this diligent writer kept himself resolutely between his people and the reader.

Here's how it might have gone if that writer had pulled back the curtain and allowed his people to step out onto the stage:

> Henshaw heard the branches parting at about the same time he heard the twig snap. He turned in time to see Chief Black Hawk and two braves step calmly into the clearing.
>
> "Chief Black Hawk," the captain said, trying to keep the surprise he felt out of his voice, "the heart of your brother is pleased to see his friend after these many summers."
>
> The chief's passive face showed no trace of emotion, but Henshaw had learned to watch the eyes; and they revealed at once the red man's amusement at Henshaw's inability to catch movement in the forest until it was too late. They regard us as children, Henshaw realized. And yet that is precisely how we regard them.
>
> Black Hawk moved with easy dignity across the clearing to Henshaw and held his hand up in greeting. "The heart of Black Hawk soars to see his old friend, the captain," he said with solemn feeling.
>
> Henshaw did not smile, though he . . .

To dramatize then, you move in close. You quote the characters and may, if you wish, allow the reader to hear not only what is spoken, but what is thought by the characters.

And you describe your people in detail as you relate precisely what they do.

As they pick up a stone, for instance, you let the reader know how it feels, its texture, and so on. And you reveal the characters' emotional reactions as they act out their roles. Think of yourself as a human camera capable of moving in so close to the people that you not only record their speech and actions, but find yourself transmitting their most private thoughts, their deepest feelings as well.

Characterization Through Dramatization

What has been covered so far is by way of underpinning the main burden of this chapter—characterization. Think for a moment about Captain Henshaw and Black Hawk as my friend presented them in his treatment of that scene he envisioned in the clearing by the river.

What understanding of them did you gain as you read his bland, distant account? Not much, certainly. However, in the rewritten version you *did* gain a more vivid picture of the captain and the chief.

In other words, characterization can best be accomplished by showing characters in action, and not by telling the reader what the characters are like. After all, we know people and we know the characters in books only to the extent that we can hear their words and observe them in action.

Think back to the characters in those short vignettes used to illustrate dramatic writing. Think of the little boy Marty. Did you get some idea of *his* character and that of his mother? Of course you did—and a much better idea than if you had had to rely on the single sentence summary.

Now, in order to develop this principle still further, let's see how the writer may characterize by simply showing a person in action—without a word of dialogue.

Jenkins strode quickly to the window of the ticket booth and slapped a ten dollar bill down on the counter, his beefy red face creasing into a boozy grin. As the ticket flickered up at him, he snatched it, grabbed the bills that were pushed toward him, and stuffed them loosely into his pocket. As he passed inside, he waved the ticket at the doorman cheerily.

Elmer moved uncertainly up to the ticket booth and

glanced at the admission price. Two dollars. Resignedly, he pulled out a crumpled dollar bill, flattened it on the counter, and pulled out a fistful of change. With careful deliberation, he counted out another dollar in nickels, dimes, and pennies and pushed the correct amount through to the ticket girl. She counted the coins deftly, then pressed the key. Elmer took his ticket, looked once more back up at the admission price, then moved toward the doorman. Taking the torn half of the ticket the doorman returned to him, he moved cautiously on into the darkness of the inner lobby.

Now obviously, these are one-dimensional characterizations, what E. M. Forster spoke of as flat characters. But they should serve to illustrate how catching someone in action can and will characterize him.

If we combine action with dialogue, we may get a still clearer picture of Jenkins and Elmer as they move on into the theater lobby.

Jenkins hurried from the men's room over to the candy counter. Glancing down at the display of candy bars, he caught sight of a Hershey bar and smiled. It was the last one in the case.

But before he could tell the blonde behind the counter what he wanted, a small voice beside him spoke up: "I'd like that Hershey bar, please."

The girl reached quickly over, retrieved the candy bar and placed it down on the counter in front of a little man standing next to Jenkins.

"Just hold on there," said Jenkins heavily. "That's my Hershey bar. I saw it first."

"I beg your pardon," said the little man, stepping back uncertainly. "Are you addressing me?"

"Well, I'm looking at you, ain't I?"

"You mean," the fellow said, "you want the Hershey bar?"

Jenkins grinned. "You catch on fast. That's the last bar and I want it. Buy something else."

The little man started to clear his throat, but before anything came out, Jenkins slapped a quarter down onto the counter, snatched up the Hershey bar, and started toward the nearest aisle.

"Keep the change, Sweetheart," he called back to the blonde.

The little man swallowed unhappily, looked nervously around him, and then pointed to another candy bar.

Certainly the action involved is not momentous: purchasing tickets and haggling over a candy bar. But after seeing and hearing these two in action, you must have come away with a definite conception of them both.

Thus, you must show your people in action. For characterization is not some magic ingredient you can inject into your people, a kind of literary adrenalin that you hope will animate your characters and thus your story with life. Characterization will take place automatically—almost accidentally—as long as you remember to show your characters doing what, for them, comes naturally.

You Must Know Your People

The only problem in using this method is that you cannot characterize your people in this fashion unless you know your characters well enough to know precisely how they will react in a given situation. If, in the middle of writing a scene, you have to pause to consider what one of your characters should do or say, stop. Go back over your notes on that character. Or prepare some. You can't create a character if you don't know that character yourself.

Sink into Jenkins' consciousness for a moment. Walk with him down the dim aisle of that theater. He is already munching on that chocolate bar as he starts into a row, his eye on a vacant seat in the center. He is anxious to sit down and watch the picture, and as a result doesn't give the little old lady sitting in the first seat a chance to get her tiny feet out of the way. He steps on one, crushing it beneath his heavy boot. The old woman cries out.

Now. What does Jenkins do? Does he apologize?

Of course not. You and I both know better than that. If he utters anything even close to an apology, it will be completely out of character.

He just mutters something unintelligible—probably a curse—and bulls his way on past that poor little old lady.

In summary, characterization is a by-product of watching people in action and hearing them speak. When they do this, they reveal who and what they are. But this means the writer *has* to know his people so well that he literally cannot imagine them doing anything "out of character." As his people come to life, as they begin to react to each other, to struggle their way to some resolution, they must choose only those options that are consistent with their character— that is, with the writer's own sure knowledge of them.

Questions for Study and Discussion

1. Do you always believe what people tell you about someone? Or do you wait to note his actions with you and with others before making up your mind? What is the legal attitude to hearsay evidence? How suspect is circumstantial evidence? How can you relate this to what this chapter has to say about the character in action?

Suggestions for Putting Your Characters on Stage

1. If that plot you roughed out still interests you, portray the main character in a typical scene that would characterize him most effectively, using action, dialogue, and an account of his thoughts as he reacts. It may help you to assume his identity yourself by writing the scene in the first person.

2. If that earlier plot treatment no longer interests you, choose another character from your notebook and dramatize him instead. Give him the full treatment: action, dialogue, some account of his thoughts.

3. For class presentation, these studies in character delineation should initiate excellent discussions, especially if the writer himself reads the scenes aloud. Hearing your words before a critical audience can be a valuable—and sobering—experience.

chapter six

Transitions

This chapter tells how to move your people from one scene into the next, how to get them from A to B — from the airport to the cabin by the lake, from the office to the train station, from Istanbul to Rome — without a stumble or a hitch — swiftly, effortlessly.

Think Scenes

First of all, you must think in terms of scenes. Even though you are not writing a play, you are building scenes as you plan and write your story or novel.

For this is what a novel or a short story is: a succession of scenes, some long, some short, all—like beads on a string—tied together by the story line. In film-making, cutting the film is a crucial art, since how the film is cut—that is, how swiftly we move from one scene to the next—is what determines its pace, a most important element. Sometimes, in fact, judicious cutting has been known to salvage an otherwise poor film, giving it a vitality and thrust it lacked before it reached the cutting room.

The Interminable Transition

Here is what sometimes happens in a beginner's story:

> "Well, that's it, boss," Jack said. "The account's settled. Anything else before I go home?"
>
> "Nothing, Jack," Collingwood said, smiling. "You've done a fine job with this account. I'll see you when you get back from the Bahamas."
>
> "Right. I'm anxious to tell Margo the good news. Two weeks in the Bahamas is a dream she's had for years."
>
> "You deserve it, Jack. Give my best to Margo."
>
> "Right," Jack said. "See you when I get back."
>
> Jack turned and walked to the door. He opened it and went out, then started along the lushly carpeted hallway to the elevators.
>
> When he came to the elevator, he pressed the small red button and stood back to wait. The elevator arrived in a moment, the door sliding open noiselessly. He stepped quickly inside and pressed the lobby button. The door closed; he felt the drop begin.
>
> At the lobby the elevator door slid open and he walked out past the newsstand and into the sunlit street. Crossing the sidewalk, he put his hand up for a taxi. Nothing happened for a while; but then a Checker taxi darted at him from out of the swarm of cars and

pulled to a stop in front of him. He got in, closed the door, and settled back in the seat.

"Grand Central," he told the driver. "I've got to catch the 4:10 to Greenwich."

The driver nodded without looking back and slammed down the flag. With a lurch the cab pulled away from the . . .

Do you think he'll ever get to Greenwich? More important, will we be with him when he does? I doubt it.

The Four Space Skip

Such interminable transitions are thoroughly unnecessary. This whole business of getting Jack from that office building to Greenwich can be handled with almost effortless despatch.

Let's go back now and do that transition over:

"Well, that's it, boss," Jack said. "The account's settled. Anything else?"

"Nothing, Jack," said Collingwood. "Fine job. See you when you get back."

"Right. I'm anxious to tell Margo the good news. Two weeks in the Bahamas! That's a dream she's had for years."

"You deserve it, Jack. And give Margo my best."

"Right. Bye now."

Jack opened the kitchen door and stepped inside. "I'm home, Margo!" he called. "Great news!"

Margo appeared in the alcove doorway, the phone in one hand, a dripping spatula in the other. "The cook's left," she snarled, "and I'm on the phone. What's all this shouting for?"

What you do is change from one scene to the next by simply skipping four spaces and commencing with the next scene. In other words, unless something vital to your story is about to take place while your hero is going from one place to another, omit all business connected with the move.

Sometimes it is helpful to indicate with dialogue or a bit of the lead character's thoughts where he is going so that when he gets there, we know precisely where he is, just as we did with Jack. We knew he was going right home to tell Margo the good news.

Let's try another transition:

"You haven't heard the last of this!" Sanford cried, stuffing the contract back into his brief case. "Chief Marshall will be most interested in this document, I can assure you."

Before Gregor could reply, Sanford turned and slammed angrily out of the office.

Chief Marshall put the contract down and looked up at Sanford, a frown on his face. "You're sure this contract is genuine?"

Sanford nodded grimly.

The chief reached quickly for his phone. "Well, well," he said, as he started dialing.

Sometimes, as well as simply moving forward in time and place, you will want to make a transition from the objective account of a character in action to his inner thoughts and concerns. Here's an example from a recent western novel of mine:

Pete dismounted also and together the two men examined the brand. There was no doubt in Joshua's mind. The brand had been altered, and it had not been a very careful or skillful job.

Joshua looked at Pete. "When we get these cattle back to grass, I want you to help me separate the Snake Bar from the Double B."

Pete looked startled. But he said nothing, just nodded.

"Good," said Joshua, swinging back onto his horse. "So let's get to it."

The beef had to be coaxed to the far end of the canyon and then worried through a long narrow gully that wound for better than one hundred yards along the base of a rock wall that leaned straight up. As Josh coaxed the brawling critters along the narrow defile, he found himself wondering for the hundredth time how creatures as useful as beef cattle could be so dumb. They had followed one steer in as he followed the sparse grass with his nose and then all of them had promptly forgotten the way out.

But then another thought occurred to Josh: perhaps these cattle had not just wandered into this canyon. . . .

The One Sentence Transition

Sometimes a one sentence transition can be managed if the time lapse is short or if the distance covered is not too great:

> Bill walked across the street and stopped in at the gas station to chat with Sam Pebbles.

The Longer Transitional Passages

And here's another transitional passage, similar to the above, but just a little more elaborate:

> Deciding it would be more politic to make his appeal to Obermeyer with no trace of whiskey on his breath, Wolf left the stable, bent down over the drinking trough's feed pump, and let the water roll into his throat and fill up his belly until it would hold no more. It had been a long dry ride.
>
> Wiping off his mouth with the back of his hand, he slapped his hat back on and walked over Snake Valley Road, along the sidewalk past the sheriff's office and into Obermeyer's. The place was cool and smelled of clean, honest implements newly minted. . . .

Of course—as hinted at in the above example—a transitional passage can be used primarily as a way to give important information to the reader. In such a case, of course, the passage would be considerably longer:

> The next season, with Jackie still in the backfield, turned out to be one of those seasons that a school dreams about as the trophies began to fill the glass case

outside the gym and the reporters started hanging around. All of a sudden, it seemed, Benson High was a power. And it was true. We didn't lose a single game that year, tying only once; and for the second year in a row we copped the conference title.

And then it was all over. Soon, all too soon it seemed, came graduation. You know how it is. First there's the Senior Prom, then the parties and the cars pulling out of the drives, everyone waving. And then summer—a sunny blur—is over, and you shoot off to all parts of the compass, some to get married, but most to jobs or college or technical school.

I went to a school of journalism in Chicago and Jackie went off with Mr. Borland and Sally to hit the speedways with that rebuilt Chevy. I was sorry to see him go. The world of racing was taking one of the greatest potential football players in the country out of circulation. That was the way I figured it anyway.

And this might have been the end of my story. But if it had been, you wouldn't be reading it. What brought Jackie back into my thoughts and finally down on paper was a phone call the middle of last August.

On the second ring I picked up the phone on my desk. "Yeah?"

"There's a young lady here to see you," Lucy told me from the switchboard. "Shall I send her in?"

"What's she want?"

As the last two examples have shown, during transitional passages you do not stay as close to the action, so to speak, as you do throughout the rest of your novel or story. Though you are still thinking in terms of scenes, you pull back, letting the narrator give a broader, wider view of the scene—a technique much like the long shot in a motion picture.

For in a novel or a story, just as in a film, the close-up view can be wearying after a while. Too *much* intensity. In short, now is the time to *tell* the reader instead of *showing*. It has to do with pace—and the need the reader has to be able to pull away from the action for a while before being plunged back into the turmoil and tension of the story's drama.

Yet you, the writer, only do this when you want to pull

back, when you feel a need to vary the pace. And the best time to do this—the most natural, at any rate—is during transitional lulls. And of course many of you will recognize that this is an excellent way to handle your openings and closings—for both are basically transitional passages.

To summarize, the guiding principle in making transitions is to make them as swiftly and as effortlessly as possible, with no straining for effect. Indeed, once the reader is aware that you are making a transition, you are in trouble. Most of the time the four space jump will handle your transition nicely.

Again, think of the films you have seen recently. Once you are well into the story, the director seldom wastes time with shots of the city, outside shots of the building with the camera panning up to the 125th floor, then a shot of the office door with the lettering, and finally a shot of the office—a common transitional method in the early days of filmmaking.

Now, very often, one scene cuts out and you find yourself well into the next scene. Since you are an intelligent human being and have been watching the action closely, it is taken for granted that you will be able to figure out from the action and the personages involved where the people are and how they got there. When you write, make your scene changes just as swiftly.

For those times in your story when you want to vary the pace, release some of the tension, choose a transitional moment, and pull back during the scene change, describing your people from a greater distance as they move on to their next challenge.

On the whole, then, don't worry about transitions . . . except when you find yourself following your lead character out of the building, down the street, through the crowd in front of Macy's, across the wide, traffic-congested avenue to the taxi-stand, where she waves fruitlessly for a while before catching the eye of a cab driver parked across the street who puts away his paper and reaches over to . . . .

Suggestions For Putting This Chapter To Work For You

1. By this time you have a few characters, at least one plot treatment using one of these characters, and some scenes in which this character is shown in action. Now would be

an excellent time to construct a few more scenes in sequence, using as many of the transitional devices mentioned in this chapter as possible.

2. Construct scenes in sequence in which the distances between each scene — in terms of both time and distance — are great. See how far you can cut into the next scene without losing your reader.

3. Bring these into class, read them to your fellow students, and see if they were able to make the jump from scene to scene easily.

chapter seven Dialogue

Dialogue gives most beginners so much trouble that they try to avoid writing it altogether, going to the extreme, in some cases, of limiting themselves to only one character. If properly assimilated, this chapter should enable you to deal with dialogue as simply one more element in our gathering conspiracy to give your fiction the illusion of life.

Fiction Talk is Different from Real Talk

In a short story or novel, just about every word must advance the story to its inevitable resolution. Dialogue is no exception. Remembering that people in fiction do not act with the same deliberateness that they do in life, you should not be surprised to find that they also do not talk in fiction as they do in life. Real people ramble unforgivably; they are appallingly indefinite. Little of this is allowed in fiction. There is simply no time for it.

Don't Ramble

Writers who mistakenly feel that they must capture every nuance of what they feel is "realistic" dialogue usually end up with something as yawn-filled as this:

> "My, don't you look nice, Edith!" Jack Winston said as he entered the old woman's room.
>
> "Thank you, Jack," she said. "It's good to see you again."
>
> Jack sat down and sighed. "I feel chilly. Where's my pipe? Ah, here it is." He took it out of his side pocket, filled it from his brown leather pouch, then struck a match and held the flame to the bowl of his pipe.
>
> Edith sat back down in her rocker by the window and took up her knitting again, though she seemed to be no longer really interested in it. "I saw Phil today. He asked about you, Jack. And Mabel. Lovely people. Sometimes I wonder if . . ."
>
> Jack had finished lighting his pipe. He leaned back in the chair and began to puff contentedly—a fragrant volcano. "Tell the squire I'll see him in the morning about those two tenants," he said to Edith. "I'll never be able to understand why he takes in such rogues. But then the squire always was a softhearted one."
>
> "I agree," Edith said. She paused and looked away from her knitting and out the window. "He certainly is." Then she looked back at him in the chair. "The squire just loves that chair, you know."
>
> "He'll miss it then, I'll wager. Yes . . . he'll miss it."
>
> She put aside her knitting resolutely. "I think I know why you are here."
>
> "You do?"

62

"Yes."

He smiled sadly and looked at his pipe.

"It's about the house," she said.

He looked up at her. "Yes, Edith. But you know I don't really want to serve this eviction notice." He looked around. "It's really *quite* chilly in here."

"We turned the heat off a bit too early this year, it seems."

He took a deep breath. "Do you want—I mean would you prefer . . . I'll come back later with this if you want."

"Here," she said, putting aside her knitting. "Let me see that notice. You do have it on you, I gather."

"Yes, I do."

"Then let me see it. We might as well see what it says, don't you think?"

He took it out of his inside jacket pocket and handed it to her. Then he relit his pipe. It had gone out. Edith began to read the eviction notice. At last she looked at him.

"This looks proper enough, I suppose. Did you have it drawn up this morning, or yesterday?"

"Well, actually . . ."

People *are* like that—especially when making decisions of this nature. They postpone coming to the point. They dawdle. They stall. During some of the most crucial scenes of their lives, they sometimes miss all the drama, all the significance of what is happening to them, as they fritter the moments away in this fashion. At times, judiciously handled, this can be very dramatic as the tension mounts. But imagine an entire story or novel written at this pace.

I usually find this sort of thing done by student writers who have read or been told that a story is fast-moving if it contains plenty of dialogue. And something like the above is their reaction. They feel that *everything* should be talked about, and at considerable length.

Telegraphic Dialogue

Then there is the other extreme. Some young writers, anxious to get on with their story and aware of the need to keep a good pace, write dialogue that sounds like a series of telegrams.

They might handle the scene with Edith and Jack in the following manner:

> Edith opened the library door. Jack entered quickly.
>
> "I have an eviction notice," he said unhappily. "I'm afraid you must sell the house and grounds, Edith! It's for your own good."
>
> Edith dissolved into tears. "But I wonder. Is it the right thing to do, Jack?"
>
> "Look. The price is a good one and life is full of change. You can't stand in the way of progress. Here's the eviction notice. Read it yourself."
>
> She took it and read it. "Yes," she said with sudden resolve. "I'll sell to your father. Have the papers ready for me this afternoon."
>
> Jack thanked her and left as quickly as he had entered.

The Illusion of Lifelike Dialogue

The trick is to give the impression of a civilized pace while mincing as few words as possible. Let's try that scene again:

> There was a knock on the library door. Edith put down her knitting, crossed the thickly carpeted floor, and pulled open the door. She was not surprised to see Jack Winston standing there, an uncertain smile on his face.
>
> "Come in, Jack," she said. "It's good to see you— even under these circumstances."
>
> He came in hesitantly. "Then you know why I'm here?" he inquired carefully.
>
> She sighed. "Yes, but it's still a pleasure to see you, Jack. Sit down."
>
> He sat in his favorite chair, the one the squire also favored, she noticed wryly. She returned to the divan and took up her knitting.
>
> "All of this business is most regrettable," she said, her eyes following the needles carefully. "Most regrettable."

Jack leaned back in the chair and looked around him at the lovely old room. It would be a shame for all this to fall before the bulldozer, but what choice did she have? He took the eviction notice out of the inside pocket of his jacket and looked at Edith. "I have the notice with me," he said gently. "Really, you must sell. The price is a good one."

"Yes," she said, glancing over at him. "I know it is." She smiled wanly, wiping away tears with the tips of her fingers. "You must forgive the tears of an old woman. This has been my home and that of my ancestors for six generations." She reached out. "Let me see that paper."

He got up and brought it over to her. She took it, her eyes suddenly cold with resolve. It took her but a few minutes to read it over. Then she looked up at him.

"They don't miss a trick, do they?"

He shook his head.

"All right. I'll sell. Have the papers ready this afternoon."

What we must have in dialogue—as in all of the action of a novel or short story—is compression, selectivity, a distillation that retains all the essentials but gives the impression that nothing has been left out—that it's all there. Once again, remember what Robert Penn Warren said: "The fictional world is *purged* of the distractions, confusions, and accidents of ordinary life." The illusion of life is what we are after, not a carbon copy.

Dialogue is no exception.

65

The Sound of Dialogue

Another problem for the beginning writer is creating lifelike dialogue that *sounds* like speech. What some write as dialogue more often than not resembles written narrative enclosed in quotation marks. It reads something like this:

... As Gulch strode across the room toward Sanderson's desk, the blind man heard his daughter leave, pulling the door shut behind her.

As soon as she had left, Sanderson turned his face in Gulch's direction. "What is the matter, Gulch? Why are you here at my ranch at this time of the day, so many miles from town?"

"Wolf Caulder has arrived in this area, Frank," the sheriff replied.

Sanderson felt a sudden dismay. But he kept his voice level. "Do you mean that you have seen him? If that is so, where did you see him?"

"No, I did not see him. But I did hear about him, and what I learned was that he had been pretty severely wounded."

"I thought you said he was here, in this area. Where is he?"

"He is now at Ellen Bowman's ranch."

"But why is he at her ranch?"

"I don't know, Frank. Bowman, her husband, rode into town late this morning. He told me and the two other men I was playing cards with that his wife had found a severely wounded man that morning in her barn and that, as soon as they had brought this wounded man into the house, she sent him on into town to get a doctor."

"Do you think it is possible that that woman might have sent for this man?"

"I do not see how she would know such a man existed, Frank. As far as I can see, the arrival of the man on her ranch was just an extraordinary coincidence."

Pretty dreadful, what? Let's try again:

66

. . . As Gulch strode across the room toward Sanderson's desk, the blind man heard his daughter leave, pulling the door shut behind her.

As soon as she had left, Sanderson turned his face in Gulch's direction.

"Well, what is it, Gulch?"

"Caulder's here, Frank."

Sanderson felt a sudden dismay. But he kept his voice level. "You've seen him?"

"No. I just heard about him. He's been shot up real bad, it looks like."

"You said he's *here.*"

"I meant at Ellen Bowman's spread."

"What the hell is he doing at her place?"

"Bowman rode in about noon. He said something about his wife finding Caulder in his barn this morning."

"Could that woman have . . . ?"

"I don't see how, Frank. It's just a crazy fluke is all."

To make the dialogue sound natural, then, you should use contractions almost exclusively and remember the *character* of the person who is speaking. In that last example, one man—the sheriff—was reporting to another man, obviously a man whose power makes him the more dominant. Also, one is less well educated than the other. The speech of both men must reflect these facts.

What is even more crucial—at least in the mechanical sense—is that the writer must not use long, involved syntax when the characters speak. Stick to short declarative sentences for the most part and do not be afraid to allow your characters to use a few sentence fragments. If you must use complex or compound sentences in your dialogue, make them short. One rule of thumb might help: If you see a semicolon in your dialogue, watch out.

Dick Tracy Dialogue

Another mistake is trying to use dialogue to convey information somewhat too obviously, so that the writer's perspiration—not his inspiration—is painfully obvious. I call this kind of dialogue *Dick Tracy dialogue*.

Here's an example:

"Not until yesterday did Thomas S. Haskins show up, Gene. I wonder why he waited so long to return."

"What was that?" asked Gene. "What did you say his full name was?"

"Thomas S. Haskins."

"How odd. That sounds like the name of the man my sister Mabel met in Burbank. It seems he sold her a phony oil well a year ago after promising to marry her. You say this man is in town visiting the Bowmans?"

"Yes, since the Wednesday before last, the fifth of April, I believe."

"You say the fifth of April? Why that's the very day that Mabel took sick and left to visit her old girl chum in Boston. Do you suppose she recognized him and left as a result?"

"Why yes, that does sound possible, at that. I remember, the Haskins fellow made a phone call the very day he arrived—and now that I think of it, he . . ."

Tiresome, isn't it? And obvious as well. Stagey. You can hear the scenery creaking. Don't do it. It is one of the worst habits you can get into, and it stems from pure bone laziness. The writer here doesn't want to go to the trouble of writing a full scene during which this critical information could be imparted gradually in the course of an interesting confrontation—one that would generate that valuable element we discussed earlier: *conflict*.

Does this mean that you should not use dialogue to convey important information to the reader? Of course not. As long as you realize that dialogue must also characterize. If at the same time you also impart information to your reader, so much the better. But dialogue that does not characterize but *only* conveys information is an opportunity missed: You kill only one bird, while the other—that of characterization— gets clean away.

Let's try again—and notice how the mental observations of the main character are used in conjunction with the dialogue to complete the picture:

"I don't believe I've seen you at the Bowman's before," said Gene pleasantly.

The garden party was a huge success. Gene already had a drink in one hand, a piece of chocolate cake in the other.

The elderly gentleman smiled graciously. He had a thick crop of white hair. That, together with his white suit, gave him a startling resemblance to Colonel Sanders. "Visiting Springdale for the first time in a long while, Mr. Steele. And it is just as I remember it as a child—an oasis in a troubled world." He sipped his tall drink and looked about him, a benign smile on his pink, freshly scrubbed face.

"Yes, an oasis it is at that," Gene replied. "We all

love it here. I don't believe I got your full name, Tom."

"Haskins," the man boomed proudly. "Thomas S. Haskins. Your servant, sir."

Gene nodded and kept his composure. He did not want Haskins to know who he was. Unless, of course, Mabel had told Haskins about him. But Mabel had been gone since the middle of April, when she had left in quite a hurry.

"Been in town long?" Gene asked.

"Since April. Got in here the fifth, as a matter of fact — just a day before my birthday."

Gene nodded and sipped his drink and forced himself to look away from the old fraud. This was the man all right. And now he knew why Mabel had left in such an all-fired hurry. He looked back at Haskins. The famous Colonel Haskins. Gene wondered what he was selling now. Snake oil?

He Said, She Said

The constant search for a word — any word, it seems — to substitute for *said* should be abandoned at once. There is nothing in the world wrong with this lovely four-letter word. Keep it. Cherish it. And don't draw attention to its absence by the use of its tiresome alternatives: *expostulated, reiterated, observed, conjectured, ejaculated, countered, remonstrated,* and others of their ilk.

The beauty of *said* is that it does its job quietly and unobtrusively: It simply tags the dialogue so the reader will know who is speaking. What is important is not the tag, but what is being said. When you replace *said* with other tags, you only draw attention to the tag itself, thus turning it into an annoying distraction.

When you wish to show emotion through dialogue and are unable to so construct your dialogue that this emotion is obvious in the words spoken, simply add a word or two to the *said:*

He said *angrily;* he said *quietly with tears in his eyes;* he said *slowly;* he said *clearly;* he said *bitterly;* and so on.

If you don't want to lean too heavily on the adverb in your writing, you could convey the needed emotion as follows:

"Never mind," he said. *He was obviously angry.*

"Yes, I know." *Paul spoke quietly with tears in his eyes.*

"Get out," she said. *Her voice had an icy clarity.*

Tyrone spoke with surprising bitterness: "Yes, I remember. Why shouldn't I?"

There are times when words such as *screamed, yelled, hooted* can be used. But always be sure *said* won't carry the load before you abandon it.

And *don't* do this:

"Where are you going?" she giggled (laughed, sang, coughed, chuckled.)

Try giggling that line, or laughing it, or singing it, or chuckling it. The way to handle this is simplicity itself:

"Where are you going?" she asked, *giggling.*

Another problem is where you put your *saids.* Again, there is really no problem at all. You can place them almost anywhere.

Before the dialogue: *Jack said,* "Where are you going? You certainly appear to be in a great hurry."

Between sentences in the dialogue: "Where are you going?" *Jack asked.* "You certainly seem to be in a great hurry."

After the dialogue: "Where are you going? You certainly appear to be in a great hurry," *Jack said.*

Sometimes you don't need the tag at all. Just make a statement concerning the speaker in the same paragraph as his dialogue. The reader will assume he is the one speaking:

Jeff turned to Phil. "I don't like this business at all. What can we do?"

"We can scream," Phil said.

Jeff turned and looked back at the farm. "Perhaps we should go back to that farm. There might be a phone we can use."

Phil laughed. "In that place?"

"It's our only hope."

"You're crazy."

Abruptly Jeff turned and started back along the dirt

road. "No, I'm not crazy. And I'm not waiting out here. I'm going back to that farm."

Phil started after him. "Come back here, you fool!"

Breaking Up Long Stretches of Dialogue

Whenever you have need of a long bit of dialogue in which one man is speaking for an extended period—a lawyer summing up his case before the jury, or the detective explaining the motivation for a crime he has just solved—break up the dialogue by having the speaker pause occasionally to look around, light his pipe, let an important point sink in. Allow those he is addressing to say something also:

Jane interrupted. "But I can't believe it!"

Inspector Brown nodded solemnly and regarded her with his sad eyes for a moment before going on: "When I saw that stain on Miss Thatcher's umbrella, I remembered the remark she had passed earlier, about leaving it home. Of course, I knew at once that . . ."

"But she *did* leave it home," Bill said, breaking in.

"Of course she did," agreed Brown, taking the pipe from his mouth. "That's just the point. You see, when I examined the umbrella, I noticed. . . ."

Indirect Dialogue

One more thing. Whenever you get a chance to use live dialogue in your writing, take it. Never use indirect or summary dialogue unless you have to, for dialogue means that people are conversing, interacting, and that's action—a possibility for conflict.

There are times, however, when indirect dialogue is acceptable. Usually, this opportunity arises when a character is relating to another person in the story something that has already been described:

"Paula!" Faith cried, falling into Paula's arms. "Thank heavens I've found you."

"I've been looking all over," Paula said. "Where on earth have you been?"

Faith looked at Paula and took a deep breath. "You won't believe it, Paula. What's happened, I mean."

"Try me," Paula said, laughing. "I just might."

So Faith told her, starting with the accident outside her apartment that morning and leaving out nothing until her lucky meeting with Paula a few moments before. When she finished, she was exhausted, but relieved—immensely relieved—that finally she had found someone to whom she could relate the whole bizarre tale.

"I believe it," Paula said cautiously. "It's so incredible."

Faith laughed.

Another time for indirect dialogue is when a difficult, perhaps tedious, technical process is being explained:

Taking the violin from her impatiently, he explained once again how to hold the bow and demonstrated the fingering with deft skill, growling unhappily at her all the while.

Still another instance when indirect dialogue is acceptable is when the speech of a character is extremely long, and unimportant portions of it need to be summarized as a welcome bit of variety:

". . . and furthermore, you must consider the other, less dramatic aspects of the psychopath's temperment, those that are, perhaps, not as exciting or as cinematographic as his more volatile traits. Yet, these, I feel, are almost equally important."

He paused then to look over his class, *and summarized again his by now familiar belief that not all psychopaths commit crimes, that most of them live lives of quiet disorder, their antisocial acts more like pranks than anything else.*

When he finished, however, he added something that caused the class to sit up with sudden interest. "Nevertheless," he said, "for all the pranksters we have in the ranks of the psychopath, we have today a growing crop of the grimmer variety—a number which is. . . .

Finally, the most important thing to remember is that dialogue does not ape the speech we use in life. Even when it seems to ramble pointlessly in fiction, it is doing so to make a valid dramatic point: Perhaps the person talking on and on is a hopeless gasbag who will never let you go once he has your ear; or maybe the disconnected dialogue indicates effects of a drug.

As your fictional characters live out their lives in the highly compressed world you create for them, the dialogue they use must reflect this compression and say what it has to say quickly and succinctly—while giving the illusion that it is unhurried and natural.

Suggestions for Putting This Chapter to Work for You

1. Go back to that notebook full of characters. Select two and allow them to engage in what could be termed a "lively conversation." Read it aloud in class.

2. Imagine two famous historical characters, say Napoleon and Washington. Dramatize them in a scene in which they discuss life and leadership and war. Perhaps they could be talking on the outskirts of hell, trying to get comfortable on a couple of large, hot stones.

3. Varying the method of tagging your speakers, create a scene between any two persons in your class. Both are very angry. They throw things. They shout. They utter obscenities. Try to convey all this with as few uses as possible of such terms as *shouted, hollered, said angrily, hissed,* and so on. Also try that method of indicating the speaker without recourse to *said* at all.

4. Go back to those people you have already placed in scenes as part of earlier assignments. Rewrite their dialogue now in the light of what this chapter has to say concerning dialogue.

    Any improvement?

chapter eight

Narrative: Locale and Action

"My task . . . is, by the power of the written word to make you hear, to make you feel—it is, before all, to make you see. That—and no more—and it is everything."

JOSEPH CONRAD

"My aim is to put down what I see and what I feel in the best and simplest way I can tell it."

ERNEST HEMINGWAY

We will examine in this chapter how place is handled, how the sights and sounds of the world you create can be presented to the reader in such a way as not to slow the dramatic pace of your story. You will then be introduced to some techniques for handling the description of fast action.

75

Those Large Chunks of Description

Some time ago, it was the style for a writer to give leisurely, quite detailed word paintings of the locale—the mountain glen, the surging city streets, the expensively furnished room. Perhaps it would be nice if today's readers would stand still long enough for such an exercise in descriptive facility, but now everything moves just a little faster than it used to—or haven't you noticed?

So—for the most part—average readers today skip right over long descriptive passages until they come to dialogue or to some other clue that the story has started up again. This creates a problem for the writer. He or she knows that locale must be included in the story, for without it the writer's characters will be acting out their drama on an empty stage.

Well, there is a solution.

Feeding in the Sights and Sounds Peripherally

Think a minute. Consider how you and I become aware of our surroundings. The sights and sounds and smells of the world around us come at us not directly, but peripherally. This, then, is the way to present the locale to the reader without slowing down the story. In other words, simply incorporate the description of the locale into the narrative, feeding it in around the dialogue and the action. This way, the reader gets the feeling of place he must have, but the story is not brought to a halt in order to provide it.

Let's look at a descriptive passage in a typical gothic romance, a genre which goes in heavily for long descriptive passages designed to build mood and suspense. In the first example the treatment is rather old-fashioned; in the second, the same material is presented in what I call the peripheral method.

> Janet stepped out onto the balcony and looked down.
>
> The view was breathtaking. Just below was the wide lawn, sweeping in gently rolling undulations all the way to the lake, leaving in its lush green wake rows of neatly trimmed hedges and squares and rectangles of brilliantly jeweled flower gardens gleaming in the late afternoon sun. And through it all wound a neat flagstone path that led down to the lakeside.

The lake itself sat in the cup of the hills like a blue platter—still, lovely, almost primordial in its beauty. And not a sail marred its surface. It was content to mirror the green lushness of the hills and the wide, azure skies above.

It was late. A soft breeze murmured through the long sad tresses of the weeping willow just beyond the balcony, and the great banks of clouds piled high in the sky almost directly overhead were touched with pink. A gull appeared from somewhere, its clean body gleaming like a pearl in the immensity of the blue heavens. Then it was gone.

Janet turned and left the balcony.

Now let's try that again:

Janet pulled away from Mark and moved out of the library and onto the balcony.

"Janet," he called after her softly, "is anything wrong?"

She did not answer him. Perhaps, she realized, it was because she did not know the answer herself. She placed both hands on the marble rail of the balcony. How old this place must be—and the memories it must hold. How many generations had Mark said?

She looked out over the grounds. The view was breathtaking. Just below was the wide lawn that swept in gentle undulations to the lake's edge. She wondered how many gardeners it took to tend the myriad flower beds the lawn had spawned, the rows of hedges, the neat winding flagstone path that led all the way down to the water.

Mark was beside her suddenly, her drink in his hand. "Here," he said softly. "You left this."

She took it from him. As she sipped it, she could not fail to notice how still and lovely the lake looked—an ironic contrast to her tumultuous feelings. Not a sail marred its surface; yet how many anxious questions stirred the surface of her emotions.

She took another sip of the claret. And then he gently removed the glass from her hand and placed it on the balcony railing. She knew what he was going to do, but felt powerless to stop him.

He turned her, and with a finger under her chin, tipped her face up gently and leaned close. The last thing she remembered seeing as he carried her from the balcony was the gull that flashed across the sky, its clean body gleaming like a pearl in the immensity of the blue heavens. . . .

In that second version, you get the picture of the estate's extensive grounds, but it is interwoven with the dialogue and the action of the scene. You also have Janet's emotions as she finds herself close to the consummation of her affair — still another dramatic factor helping to add spice to the passage. Furthermore, the descriptive material itself is a great help in establishing the girl's mood as the calm scene below the balcony becomes an ironic contrast to her feelings at the moment.

Another thing: The first version was almost entirely something someone would see, not feel. It was too impersonal — too much like an inventory — to make you feel close to it. But when the description is integrated with the scene, the writer is more likely to bring in senses other than that of sight. In this case the sense was touch, as when Janet touched the cold marble of the railing. This sensory impression was lacking in the first chunk of description. It helps greatly to enlist the aid of as many of the senses as you can; and this — it turns out — is much easier to do when the background is integrated into one smoothly flowing unit of narration.

The Tendency to Overwrite

78

Perhaps you noticed something else. In the first version there were too many words, too many descriptive adjectives. The reader was being *told* too much. And that's because this old-fashioned way of presenting the locale had a dangerous fascination for the writer. He tended to lose control, to overwrite, to allow himself too many liberties in terms of vocabulary, metaphor, and sentence structure. And what he became was a bore.

Did you notice, also, the *pathetic fallacies:*

It (the lake) was content to mirror the green lushness of the hills and the wide, azure skies above.

A soft breeze murmured through the long sad *tresses of the weeping willow. . . .*

The *pathetic fallacy* is the habit some poets and beginning writers have of endowing trees, flowers, clouds, stones, rocks, and hills with human traits and feelings It is a trap difficult to avoid, but avoid it the writer must. Again, this trap is all the more difficult to escape when the writer begins to indulge him or herself with long, poetic, descriptive passages.

Indeed, even metaphors and similes should be regarded with suspicion by the careful writer. They muddy more often than they clarify; and nothing is so completely awry, it seems, as a metaphor that has gotten itself all mixed up—Joyce Kilmer's notorious tree is only the most obvious example. Basically, the metaphor and the simile are liberties taken with the truth in an effort to gain a sharper, more dramatic picture. But no matter how much they are favored by those who prefer to think of writers as stylists first and story tellers second, they distract. And when a writer's style attracts attention to itself in that manner, the style has failed.

In Hemingway's *Big Two-Hearted River*—a superb celebration of the outdoors and one young man's kinship with it—few if any metaphors or similes are employed by the writer, one whose style has done more than any other to strip the barnacles from our prose.

Of course, descriptive passages without an occasional simile or metaphor can become pretty arid at times. But it is always better to err on the side of too little rather than too much. As for the *pathetic fallacy*, there is never a time when it can be employed to any honest advantage in descriptive passages. Fortunately, descriptions of locale interwoven with the action act as an effective brake on this kind of indulgence. Since the scene must be kept moving, the writer's red pencil is kept active, and the writer finds that all those lovely words are simply not needed in order to get the job done.

When Do You Describe Locale?

The answer is whenever the locale itself is important to the story you are telling. This means that descriptions of locale are not just stuck anywhere in the novel or story to impress the reader. Like everything else in your narrative, the locale has important functions to perform.

What are some of those functions? Obviously, you will want to describe the background of any new place where your people find themselves acting out their drama. The beginning of a novel usually calls for descriptive passages. When introducing a new character in a narrative, it can sometimes be done quite effectively by placing that character against a background that will help in his characterization. And finally, whenever the locale or background itself becomes a menacing or crucial element in the development of the story, that locale must be described.

Beginning a novel:

Wolf Caulder reined in his black and let his gaze sweep over the lush grasslands that opened up before him. He had just come through a pass and was looking down now at a broad valley with a wide creek snaking through the center of it, willows lining the bank. The entire valley floor was a sea of grass, the fragrant wind rippling it like water. And far below, barely visible from where Wolf sat his horse, a small nest of cabins and corrals had been set in among a stand of cottonwood.

Profoundly relieved to be quitting the parched land behind him, Wolf urged his black on down the slope toward the distant cluster of buildings. Soon he was riding through grass that reached to his stirrups, the odor of sage clouding his senses.

When he was close enough, he was able to see a thin tracery of woodsmoke lifting from the chimney of the largest log house. Fine. That would mean coffee at least. A brook feeding into the creek crossed his path and he pulled his black up gently and eased him into the soft mud around it.

The shot came as the horse stepped carefully down into the brook's channel. . . .

Introducing a new character:

Frank Sanderson sat facing the open window, the bright sun slanting across his seamed face, down his vest, and over his left forearm. He liked to sit in the sun like this, drinking in the smells that came in the open window—especially the pungent odor that came from the sun-baked grease on the wagon wheel someone must have left just outside the window.

From the way sound carried and the feel of the sunlight on his face, he had little trouble imagining the sky's cobalt blue and the white glare of the hard-packed front yard before the main corral. But it was his ears that brought the scene to life for him: the lazy shuffle of his cowpokes as they went about their business and the nervous hooves of the broncs circling inside the corral; while above it all the steady clangor from the blacksmith shop off to his left brought to his mind's eye a picture of the bright white flame guttering in the bellow's blast and the rippling muscles of his giant of a blacksmith as the man brought down his hammer. . . .

Breaking suddenly into this came the sound of his daughter's boots as she strode quickly across the yard toward the ranchhouse. She passed just in front of his open window, mounted the low porch, and entered the house. Sanderson swung his swivel chair about and directed his sightless gaze at the door a moment before he heard it swing open.

"What is it, Laura?" he asked.

The locale as menace:

The trail followed the crest of the ridge, which shouldered higher and higher, at last affording Cal a spectacular view of the mountain range. Far off to his right the gleaming band of silver that was Indian River wound its way through defiles and narrow canyons, and beyond it—on the other side of Bridger Peak—gleamed the blue cup of water that was Indian Lake, out of which spilled the river.

To his left he saw only badlands, peaks, and ravines, with Horsehead looming over it all. From this angle the peak no longer resembled the head of a horse, but it dominated the landscape completely. And then Cal was noting the trail ahead of him. It appeared to drop out of sight. He pulled up and then gently coaxed his horse to the lip of the ridge. As soon as he neared the edge, he found the trail again swinging off to his left, winding close around a huge boulder.

The trail dropped off swiftly then—almost too steeply—before leveling off. In that instant Cal got a quick glimpse of a green land far below, surrounded on all sides by precipitous walls. Abruptly as he rode on, the jutting fingers of rock closed off the view. But Cal knew now where he was heading: into a hidden valley that only a rider with a map—or a fresh pair of tracks to follow—could have found.

Know What You Describe

When it comes to describing locale, you had better know the places you are describing pretty well. If you have never been to Arabia, for instance, don't rely on the movies you've seen to give you the feel for the background you'll need for a story dealing with a typical Arabian. You just don't know enough—and it would take an enormous amount of time to research the background well enough to write about it convincingly.

This is why some historical novels have a static quality about them, like ponderous oriental tapestries, moving heavily and sluggishly in the wind of your comprehension. This is not to say that locale in historical fiction cannot be well done. A writer can imagine and do almost anything his genius allows—but why saddle yourself with an almost insurmountable problem of research in your first efforts as a writer?

In fact, once you start writing, you will find that you don't really know *any* locale as well as you thought you did. This means you will find yourself constantly engaged in research. There is no way to get around it, for if you are going to implant a locale in the mind's eye of your reader, you'd better have it already implanted in your own.

Get to know your local librarian. She in turn will acquaint you with the atlases, *The National Geographic, Webster's Geographical Dictionary*, the encyclopaedias, and with many other invaluable reference books. In addition, she will perhaps know many of the books—fiction and nonfiction—by those experts who have been there. Don't overlook another major source. It is sometimes the quickest and surest way to find out what you need to know about a place. Pick up the phone and call an expert.

Again, however you research your locale, do it. You

must. It will add a dimension your narrative must have if it is to stand. Irving Stone worked for a while in a marble quarry in Italy as he researched his novel *The Agony and The Ecstasy;* and James Hilton poured over National Geographics to gain the sense of place he needed to describe his Tibetan world in *Lost Horizon.*

Visualization

Your visualization will be poor at first. It will improve only with practice. Some writers visualize very well, others poorly. But they manage to get by. They still see enough of what they are describing so the lack of any great keenness of perception is seldom missed.

I refer you to the mystery novels of Erle Stanley Gardner. His visualization of locale is somewhat skimpy. But he didn't seem to have any difficulty in giving us a pretty clear picture of Perry Mason and Della Street.

Take Your Time

You know and I know that when two cars meet in a collision, it is all over in an instant. Yet if you were to describe all of the things that happened to those two automobiles at the moment of impact, it would most likely take an hour to read. Alas, you say, it can't be done. How can you get it all in, and still make it seem as if it happened in an instant?

Whenever you describe complicated, fast action, forget the element of time while you are doing so. Just select judiciously and do as good a job as you can of making clear what happened, giving the reader only occasional statements as to how much time has elapsed:

> The two cars were traveling at speeds slightly in excess of sixty miles an hour. The blue Chevy struck the left side of Will's Ford and drove it to the right and off the road, causing it to flip over as it struck the guardrail. The Chevy ground on, catapulting over the Ford, turning a complete somersault in midair as it did and landing— incredibly—on all four wheels in the field beyond.
>
> Will's Ford continued to roll over and over; and before it came to a halt upright, there was a muffled explosion. A sheet of bright orange flame enveloped the

crumpled hood. The blue Chevy, remaining upright, charged like a demented bull across the field until it buried its snout into the base of a massive oak.

It did not burst into flame. It just disintegrated and sagged forward, while the sound of rending metal and shattering glass filled the air. The hood, the motor, the front wheels all seemed to have been swallowed up by the tree. The windshield disappeared in a twinkling. The roof shrank down upon the body, transforming the side windows into bent trapezoids of shattered glass.

Before the tinkle of broken glass had died, the sound of water sizzling on hot metal came sharply across the clearing, punctuating the sudden, stunned silence. But the silence lasted only an instant as it was violated by the ragged chorus of screams that came from the occupants of both cars.

And Will's cry, broken and hoarse, cut through all the others: "I'm burning! I'm burning! Oh, my God! I'm burning!"

In short, by taking your time and telling as directly as you can all that you can recall of the image you have in your head, you'll do the job. Remember, you don't tell everything. You select. But you relate the sequence—no matter how complicated—with a care designed to catch each single step in the gathering crescendo of action, thus reducing the seeming chaos of the action to a logic and a coherence your reader will need to have in order to visualize it clearly. Do all this confident that your reader will know the action is transpiring in only a few seconds, even though there is a measurable lapse of time for its description, a lapse definitely in excess of the time it takes for the action to complete itself.

That last example described a complicated action from a distance. The sequence might make an acceptable opening for a story or a novel; but once most writers get inside their story they usually describe violent action as it affects a single person, zooming the camera in closer, so to speak:

Christopher didn't see the roller skate. He just felt it as it flew out from under his foot, his foot going along for a good part of the ride. The rest of him followed: his right leg shooting out first, followed by his rear end and torso as he sailed into the air and out over the stairs.

He was in flight for only an instant and was surprised at the suddenness with which the bannister changed its direction in relation to his head. His left shoulder struck the stair first. It went numb instantly, as if something had switched off all the feeling in that portion of his anatomy. Then a sharp pain coursed up his leg from his left ankle, and he felt that sickening sense you get when you feel a bone snap.

He heard himself scream out in pain and outrage, furious that something as banal as Freddy leaving his skate on the top step could do all this to him. Then he thumped clumsily, ludicrously down the stairs into an absurd, frightening darkness. . . .

To sum up this chapter: For the most part, long descriptive passages are out. You will find it more effective to feed your locale in with the action of your story so that it does not slow the pace of the narrative. Some knowledge of your locale — however acquired — is needed if you are to visualize accurately in your mind's eye what you are planning to put down on paper. But don't be disturbed if your visualization is poor as you begin to write; it will get better. If it doesn't, you may still be able to write successfully. Action, or perhaps characterization, will be your strong points, rather than your ability to evoke a particular place.

When describing action, simply tell what happens clearly and cleanly. Don't try to include everything that happens. Select judiciously, so as to present a clear picture to the reader, and do this without trying to color your account with adjectives or adverbs. It is enough if your reader can clearly see what happens. As for the element of time, indicate the time elapsing as you describe the sequence of events, allowing the reader to realize for himself — as he will — that the time it takes to relate the action and the time elapsed for the action itself will not necessarily be the same.

When describing locale and fast action, the closer you weave these elements to your characters, the greater will be the dramatic impact of what you write. Finally, do not overwrite. Get by with as little fancy writing as your ego will permit. Word painting can get to be pretty intoxicating at times, so stay on the wagon and keep your prose sober. Concentrate on describing the concrete as clearly and simply as you can. Your job, as that very great writer Joseph Conrad pointed out, is to make your reader see what you see—not to impress him with your style.

Suggestions for Putting This Chapter to Work for You

1. Select a news item from your local newspaper—automobile accident, gas main explosion, riot—and describe it, first as an observer close by and then as a participant in the action.

2. Describe a specific restaurant or bar near your home by incorporating it into a scene involving two lovers. Or describe a brawl within its confines. Or how it sleeps on an early Sunday afternoon.

3. Go back to that plot treatment. Select a sequence that will necessitate some detailed description of the locale and dramatize it.

     Then keep it for the future.

chapter nine **Flashback**

I hope that in this chapter you will receive some help in deciding when and how to use the full-blown flashback as well as some examples of how you may feed antecedent material into the narrative without bringing the forward progress of your story to a halt.

His Thoughts Returned to ...

In many stories or novels, those crucial events that have helped to make your characters what they are may already have taken place. The trouble is that these events are back where you can't get your hands on them easily—and now you need your reader's awareness of them in order to make clear to him what is happening or about to happen in your story.

One solution is to go back:

> His thoughts returned to that incredible afternoon ten years before when first he met her. He could almost hear her again—calling to him across that field. It was a Sunday. He'd been up all that previous night . . .

And so on. You stop the story and take the reader back along with you. The trouble is that sometimes your reader would rather not make that trip; he'd rather go on with the story. As a result, you lose him. For this reason, you should think twice before writing the flashback.

Is This Trip Necessary?

Look at it this way. If what happened long ago is so important and exciting that it will add vital interest and meaning to your story, why not start back there in the first place? Tell it vividly. Then jump ahead to the time of your story and proceed from there. You could write the segment as a short, introductory paragraph to your story, or as an italicized opening portion of your first chapter. However you do it, you will be including the needed material, but your forward momentum will not be sacrificed.

What you'll probably find, actually, is that you don't need to use a full-scale flashback, that the information can be fed in gradually during the course of the narrative.

To illustrate this point, let us go first to the full-scale flashback, then show how this same material can be fed into the narrative without the use of the flashback:

> Martin flipped off the intercom, got up and went to the window. Paul Scranton—his wife Elaine's cousin— was on his way up. And Scranton had no idea that Janet had been his kid sister.

As he stood there at the window, he found himself back in the doorway of that small furnished room, straining to see in the dim light.

"Janet," he had called softly. "Janet. Is that you?"

"Yes." Her voice was ragged, hopeless.

He closed the door behind him. Janet was lying face down across the bed, the phone in her hand. She turned to look at him, her face swollen from crying.

He moved to her side, took the phone from her hand and lifted it to his ear. "You still there, Janet?" came a cold voice. "Now listen. You know you got yourself into this. You had your fun too, don't forget. We both got our kicks. But the game's over now. I'll swear the kid's not mine. So get an abortion. Don't be a sap. So long. It was real nice knowing you." He hung up.

"Who was that?" Martin asked tightly, surprised at the control in his voice.

"Paul," Janet said dully. "Paul Scranton."

He put the phone down and sat beside her on the bed and placed his hand on the small of her back. "Look, sis. If you want the kid, keep it. If not, see me. Together we can handle this thing. Forget that crumb."

"I already have," she said. He didn't like the sound of her voice.

"Come on, sis. We're getting out of here. This is no place for you."

She rolled away from him. "Leave me alone, Marty. I'm all right. I'm over 21. Just let me handle this, will you?"

He got up and looked down at her. "I want to help. Let me."

"I don't *want* you to help. This is my life, Marty. Thanks. But no thanks."

He felt drained; looking down at her, he suddenly realized how little control he had over those forces that touched the people he loved. Always he'd tried to save Janet from . . . this sort of thing . . . from guys like Paul Scranton. But now he saw how helpless he was—had always been.

"All right," he said, his voice tight. "But give me a call if you need anything—anything at all. Please." He

89

opened his wallet and dropped some bills onto the bed. "Here. Get yourself a nicer place than this. Do that much for me anyway."

She smiled wanly. "Sure, Marty. I promise. Now get out of here. I'm a mess."

So he had left her in that room. Perhaps he should have insisted that she come with him, but he hadn't. And later Janet went to some butcher for the abortion. The operation had been botched cruelly, and Janet had died in a cheap, evil-smelling room across town.

And now he was about to meet this same Paul Scranton face to face. He turned from the window just as the door opened. Scranton entered swiftly, a cocky smile on his face, his hand extended. Martin shook it and indicated a leather chair next to his desk.

Scranton sat down. "Thanks for seeing me."

"Elaine had some fine things to say about you, Paul. She wanted me to help—to see if I couldn't place you somewhere."

"That's awfully decent of her."

"Been in New York long?"

"Just got in."

"What made you ring Elaine?"

He smiled. "When a guy needs a friend, that's Elaine."

"Of course."

"And I knew her pretty well in college."

Martin caught the hint of something in that statement and tightened. All right. He would help this fellow. He would help him good. He leaned forward in his seat.

"I do have a job," he began. "It's not exactly the easiest. . . ."

Feeding in Antecedent Material

Now let's feed this bit of antecedent material in with the narrative:

Martin flipped the intercom. Scranton was on his way up. He had promised Elaine he would help him, but since the moment he had realized who Paul Scranton was, he had known he would be unable to keep that promise. How could he forget what Scranton had done to his kid sister? The odd thing was that Scranton apparently had no idea he knew.

He got up as Scranton entered swiftly, confidently, a cocky smile on his face, his hand extended. Martin shook the offered hand and indicated the leather chair next to his desk.

Scranton sat down. "Thanks for seeing me."

"Elaine had some fine things to say about you, Paul. She wanted me to help—to see if I couldn't place you somewhere."

"That's awfully decent of her."

Yes. Martin remembered that voice—so hard and smooth. He had heard it three years before when he had taken a phone from his sister's hand as she lay face down on an unmade bed in a dingy furnished room. Lifting the phone to his ear, he heard that cold voice—heard its chill, rasping brutality:

You got yourself into this, kid. You had your fun and games, and I had mine. I'll swear it's not my kid. Get an abortion. Don't be a sap. So long. It was real nice knowing you.

And then had come the harsh click of the dead phone.

Janet got the abortion; but it was botched cruelly. She had died in a cheap, evil-smelling room somewhere across town.

"Been in New York long?" Martin asked.

"Just got in."

"What made you ring Elaine?"

He smiled. "When a guy needs a friend—that's Elaine."

"Of course."

"And I knew her pretty well in college."

Martin caught the hint of something in that statement and tightened. All right. He would help this fellow. He would help him good. He leaned forward in his seat.

"I do have a job," he began. "It's not exactly the easiest. . . ."

91

In this second version the reader gets the information he needs, and he is certainly made aware of the anguish the hero feels; but it is all part of the present scene, integrated into the narrative so smoothly that the action is hardly slowed at all.

In fact isn't this how the past acts on us all—as occasional shards invading the fabric of our present—giving sudden poignancy to an otherwise casual encounter? As we move down the streets of our lives, we have with us as constant companions the ghosts of those people and events that once were a part of our present. We get them back in fugitive bits and pieces, never as full-blown episodes. If our aim, then, is to capture in fiction the illusion of life, handling antecedent material in the manner shown in the second example seems to be the wisest course.

All Right Then: Go Back

Nevertheless, there will be times when you simply have to devote a small passage or a chapter or two to the past. You can recall novels or short stories, I am sure, in which flashbacks were used quite effectively.

Well then, how do you know when you should use the full flashback? When, no matter how skillful you are at feeding in antecedent material, you find you have not been able to impart to the reader enough of what he must know. Perhaps the material of the flashback is so dramatic, so filled with the conflict your story needs at this point that you simply can't throw away this material. And then again the information contained in the flashback may be absolutely crucial to an understanding of the lead character's motivation.

All right, then. Go back:

Ben was asleep in the cabin loft and Will was sitting atop the corral fence, having a solitary smoke. The sight of Josh for the second time that day had sent his thoughts back.

He had told Josh he was in this high country because of a promise he had made to someone. Yes, but not a promise he had made to Pike Johnson—as Josh undoubtedly thought. No, Will's promise had been to Kathy Blackmann, to Josh's mother.

With a quick sweep of her pale hand, Kathy caught the luxuriant fullness of her auburn hair and sent it cascading back down over her bare shoulders. "I want to see him, Will! I want to go back just once and see him on a horse. I want to watch him ride—see him smile. Will, he's got the finest, most honest smile. Honest to God, he has!"

"I believe you," he said, laughing and pulling her to him, cradling her naked shoulders and breasts in his own naked arms. He kissed her lightly on the tip of her nose—a strong handsome nose, nothing cute about it.

He pulled back and looked at her. Her dark powerful eyes burned like coals in her flushed cheeks. With a sudden ache Will realized how sick she was—what a terrible lie those flushed cheeks were. Kathy Blackmann was dying. She knew it. Josie knew it. They all knew it, but said nothing. He kissed her suddenly on the lips and drank deep, her warmth filling him, renewing him.

"You're not listening," she said, a hint of despair in her voice as her lips left his.

"Yes, I am, Kathy."

She sighed. "I wrote Josh's father. I asked him if I could come back for just a visit. He wouldn't allow it. He wants me to stay dead. I know what he must have told Josh—that I ran off with that poor slip of a cow hand."

"Maybe you should write Josh—tell him the truth. Tell him what really happened."

She frowned and turned away. "No. It would turn Josh against his father. And right now that's all he's got. He loves his father, admires him—and someday that empire John's building will belong to Josh. I want that for him. If I did anything now to upset that it would leave him with nothing."

Will took her in his arms again, astonished as always by the tenacity and depth of a mother's love for her own. "All right," he said. "Don't write him, then. Just get better, that's all."

She nodded solemnly at that, then pulled away and looked up into his face. "Will, promise me one thing?"

"Name it."

"If ... well, if anything were to happen to me,

93

*would you go back ... I mean to see how Josh is getting
on ... to see that he doesn't ... well, let his father's
brutality take all the gentleness — all the kindness out of
him?"*

"That's a tall order, Kathy."

"I trust you, Will."

*"It's a promise. But nothing's going to happen to
you, Kathy. You're going to be back helping Josie run
this place before long. You'll see. Now, come here — before Josie comes back in with some more of that damn
medicine of hers."*

*Willingly, her dark eyes smoldering, Kathy raised
her face to his. ...*

Will flicked his cigarette away into the gathering
twilight, recalling with a dull ache the pitiless, relent-
less speed with which Kathy's dread illness consumed
her — leaving him with only his memory of her and of
his promise.

If the material in this flashback had been fed bit by bit
into the ongoing narrative as suggested earlier, it would have
been very difficult for the writer to capture the essence of
that scene, which was this man's love for the woman and
her love for her son. Meanwhile, of course, much additional
antecedent material pertaining to this woman's story will
still need to be fed into the narrative both before and after
this flashback.

Notice the use of italics. This enabled the writer to dispense with the use of *had* in the opening of the flashback
and plunge the reader instantly backward in time so that the
immediacy of the scene is enhanced, thus taking the curse
off the fact that all this happened in the past.

This is an important factor, since once you decide to go
back you must exploit to the hilt the flashback's full dramatic potential and write the episode as vividly as you
would write about an event taking place in the present.
Think of it as present, in fact. This will help.

If you choose not to use italics throughout the flashback — and it would not be a good idea if the flashback were
any longer than the one I quoted — simply skip four spaces

and proceed as in the first example given in this chapter. Start off, using *had* with your verbs for a while to indicate to the reader that this has all happened before. But since the objectionable feature of the flashback is that the reader knows it has all happened in the past, dispense with *had* as soon as possible. Keep *had* for the first sentence of the flashback only. When you return to the present, you may indicate this by using *had* again; but remember, use this helping verb sparingly:

When Tom at last tried his arm under the beneficent heat of the Florida sun, he found that his arm had not been convinced by his catcher's trusting diagnosis. His shoulder had bothered him with the first pitch. Yet, at that point, the pain had not been something he couldn't grit through, so he said nothing more about it and had begun to pitch regularly.

Now, as Tom waited in the empty little office, his aching shoulder a constant reminder of the game he had just lost, he felt that he was slipping into a nightmare from which there was no chance of waking. . . .

In summary, try not to rely on the flashback for antecedent material that you might better feed into your ongoing narrative. If, however, you feel that you will gain more than you will lose by stopping the narrative and going back, then do so.

But always ask yourself: Is this trip necessary?

Putting This Chapter to Work for You

1. Write an extensive scene—possibly from that plot treatment you wrote earlier—including in the scene a full-scale flashback—the whole bit: description, background, dialogue. A scene from the character's childhood is a natural, say, for example, the first time he did something or other. Then again, it could be some traumatic episode that has colored his life ever since.

2. Rewrite the scene now, fitting the material of the flashback into the present scene as was done in the example included in this chapter.

3. Read both versions to your classmates and let them decide which version is best. Or let your instructor read both versions and make this judgment.

chapter ten **Point of View**

It is time now for you to become acquainted with the various viewpoints from which the story you are telling can be experienced by the reader. Since each story or novel has to be told from whatever point of view best suits that particular story, helping you judge correctly which vantage point would be most effective is one of the chief considerations of this chapter.

You Must Have a Vantage Point

The *point of view* is that vantage point from which the writer relates the action of his characters and from which the reader, therefore, is forced to view the proceedings. As you prepare to tell your story, you must decide where you and your reader will be standing as the events of your tale unfold. Will you be inside the consciousness of the main character, and none other? Will you be a friendly observer who knows all of the principals very well, but none intimately? Or perhaps you will be a God-like intelligence hovering over the scenes and the characters of your story, flitting from one personality to another. Then again, maybe it all happened to you, and now you are telling the reader exactly how it was.

Whichever point of view you select, you must do so on the basis of its fitness for the narrative you wish to relate. In order to make this judgment intelligently, you should know both the advantages and the disadvantages of each viewpoint. Let's take them one at a time:

First Person

Most readers and most beginning writers feel perfectly at home with the first person point of view; and it is a fairly serviceable viewpoint with a long and honorable career. Remember *Treasure Island? David Copperfield? A Farewell to Arms?* For achieving unity and believability, there is probably no other point of view that surpasses it.

The writer simply relates what happens to his main character as if he were the main character. It is a relatively simple thing to imagine oneself as the hero of one's daydreams and then put it all down just as it happens. The reader following such an account has little difficulty identifying with the hero, of course, and this is why the believability quotient is so high with this viewpoint.

The trouble with the first person point of view, however, is that the reader never really sees the main character — from the outside, that is. As a result, the writer is usually reduced to all sorts of creaky ploys to get some account of his main character's appearance across to the reader.

I'm sure you've read them. The heroine decides to comb her hair. Before you know it, she's describing the shape of her mouth and the impish light in her green eyes.

Let's take another example:

98

I put down the paper and glanced out at the Swiss countryside stroking past the window. It was pleasant, and for a moment I relaxed. Suddenly the train entered a tunnel.

The green world vanished and in its place I saw a tired man of forty-three staring at me. I looked back. My broad-brimmed hat was out of style, my face unusually haggard, with eyes like sunken coals. There were deep lines about my mouth, and my full mustache needed trimming.

Yes, I looked like hell—and that was precisely how I felt.

I went back to my paper and did not look up when the bright world returned, but kept on reading until I reached Zürich.

The writer almost has to resort to these devices in order to give substance and reality to his lead character. Otherwise, the hero seems but a disembodied presence—alert, humorous, capable of feeling pain and enjoying laughter, and yet, through it all, having no more real presence than a wreath of smoke.

Nevertheless, this point of view remains a very effective viewpoint, especially because of the ease with which it enables the reader to identify with the main protagonist, a factor which always increases the emotional power of what you are writing:

The first icy shock of the cove's waters was only partially softened by the vest; and then I cut through the water, submerged completely, forcing myself to adjust to the cold. The green, shimmering encasement of water pushed in upon me as I shot for the bottom, my flippers working perfectly as they propelled me almost effortlessly.

I straightened at last and ran along the bottom of the cove. A small flotilla of striped bass and a school of bluefish flickered past me. I paid no attention as I scanned the dim, silty sea bottom. Cilia-like seaweed undulated sluggishly as I passed. A male stickleback, on guard over his nest of weeds, darted warningly up to me, then flicked aside.

A large bass cut at right angles to my course only a few feet below me. It was a magnificent specimen. I turned my head to follow its path — and caught sight of something else. At once I changed direction and circled warily in the direction the fish had taken. When I was directly over it, I folded down quickly and kicked.

What I saw as I got closer was an enormous fish of some kind, roughly triangular in shape, that seemed to be resting on the bottom of the cove alongside what looked like a deep trench.

For the first time I felt fear.

Notice how easy it is to identify with that diver, to feel and see what he feels and sees. This is one reason why this point of view is preferred in those stories and novels where identification with the hero or heroine is wanted above all else: gothic tales, mysteries, adventure tales. I remember how my heart sank when, reading *Treasure Island*, I felt that fearsome blind man Pew's hand as he snatched my wrist and drew me close. For *I* was Jack Hawkins as I read that marvelous adventure tale. First person narration has this ability to pull you into the story in that fashion, as I am sure you know from your own reading.

Unity and believability, then, as well as ease of reader identification are the great advantages of this point of view. Its only significant drawback, I repeat, is the difficulty it presents in portraying the protagonist visually. In addition, there is also the danger of making your main character sound somewhat self-centered and not a little boastful as he recounts his adventures and as the number of first person singulars beats upon the reader's consciousness in a steady, seemingly interminable drumfire.

This, of course, is something you will have to watch carefully.

The Frame Within a Frame

A variant on the first person point of view is the frame within a frame, where someone tells the story to listeners or a friend sitting across from him at a kitchen table, and the writer's narration introduces this scene to the reader. Joseph Conrad was the most successful practitioner of this device. Few since have been able to approach his mastery of the frame within a frame. But the fact is that in too many stories using this technique the introductory frame—that is, the fireside or the front porch, the group of hushed listeners, the voice of the speaker, and so on—is simply not needed. The writer would have been just as well off if he had dispensed with the entire business and begun where the narrator begins—at the beginning of the story.

At any rate, the frame within a frame is seldom employed today, since it tends to creak a little in the hands of those who do not really need to tell their story in this fashion. However, it is still a serviceable device when properly used—that is, with the elaborate frame missing and only the narrator's voice retained.

Undoubtedly, Jack Schaefer's *Shane* was the success it was almost entirely due to Schaefer's use of this device. The story, in essence, was the classic western myth: a lone horseman riding into a western town, a decent man reluctant to use his gun again, but forced at last to face down the hired gun, and then to ride on and out of the lives of those he has touched—and altered. The story has been written countless times and will continue to be written well into the foreseeable future; but what gave *Shane* its special, enduring quality was the fact that it was narrated by the participant in the action—a young boy at the time, grown now and pondering the events and their meaning as he relates to the reader what happened.

If you are certain that, in order for the events of your story to realize their full dramatic potential, they must be filtered through the personality of an onstage narrator, go ahead and use the device. But dispense with the "frame." Just begin at the beginning:

> If Jackie Shaw had been coming straight at you in those days, you would have thought he was about to run over you. Often, he had a sullen, almost glowering look, accentuated by his broad brow and square jaw and the resolute thrust of his shoulders.
>
> But then, as soon as he saw you, he'd smile. The effect was immediate, like the sun coming out from behind a bank of clouds. Of course, it wasn't really all that dramatic, you understand. But the change was remarkable, for Jackie was a moody sort, full of quick changes of disposition. Yet, once you got to know him, it was worth it.
>
> I'm the *Times-Herald* sports editor now, but in those days I was the manager of the Benson High Foot-

ball team, and I was on hand the first day Jackie showed up for practice. I was sitting on the bench, my bucket of water in front of me as I watched the team work out.

The air was crisp, and the sound of footballs thunking to the turf and shoulder pads clashing came clearly across the field to where I was sitting. I guess you might say I had been waiting all summer for the season to begin, and now that it had, I was content. I didn't hear any footsteps behind me; so it was completely without warning when a heavy hand came down hard upon my back.

I turned suddenly and found myself looking up into Jackie Shaw's broad, grinning face. This was the first time. . . .

From this point on the narrator-observer keeps close tabs on the main character and tells his story in the process. He cannot relate to the reader, of course, those events he does not witness, and this can be an advantage, helping to build suspense as both the reader and the narrator speculate on the true motives of the characters and what is happening to them.

Later on in the story we get passages that might sound like this:

About a week later during practice, I happened to look up and see Jackie talking to the coach. He was not in uniform and was carrying a load of books. Sally was standing on the grass well back of the bench waiting for him. When I caught her eye, she waved and I waved back.

The conversation was a short one, and at its conclusion Jackie stepped back with a smile on his face and shook the coach's hand. It looked as if they had buried the hatchet finally, and I wondered if this meant Jackie would start showing up for practice again. As he walked off the field with Sally, I reminded myself that I should give him a call when I got home that night.

I never got around to doing so, but as it turned out, the call would have been unnecessary. Jackie showed up in full uniform the next day, and the coach worked him . . .

In this segment the narrator is kept back. He doesn't

hear what the coach and the hero say to each other and is left—like the reader—to speculate on what transpired in that short conference.

But he can, however, move in closer to the action:

> Sally's father had already climbed out through the side window, and he yelled at us to get extinguishers. Jackie pulled up at once, and the two of them raced back to the pits. I pulled up beside Sally and waited for them to return. By this time the front of the car was completely enveloped in flames.
>
> I held up my arm to protect my face and moved back with Sally as Jackie and Mr. Borland brought the fire under control. Both front tires were puddles of evil-smelling rubber by this time, and the entire hood of the car was twisted and blackened.
>
> I shook my head as Jackie and Mr. Borland returned to us with their spent extinguishers. "Too bad," I said. "All that work."

And here, with the frame completed, is how this story might end:

> At the beginning of this story I said that getting to know Jackie was what this story was all about. I wanted you to know and to like him as I did and, if possible, to see what it was that made him the way he was. But now that I'm finished, I don't know if I've succeeded. It's not possible, I guess, to ever know another man completely, to put all the pieces neatly together and say, "Here it is. Now you know him."
>
> But if you've followed the sports pages since that exhibition game last August, you've heard about Jackie Shaw, and you know that he must be a man in complete control. And if this is so, it is my feeling that Jackie Shaw first came to know himself—and thus learned to govern himself—during that difficult season back when he was Benson High's fullback fury.

103

What this point of view gives the writer is a chance to speculate, to pull back conveniently when it best serves his purposes and—most important—to allow for some ambiguity in his presentation of the character and perhaps also in the events of the story. If this is the effect the writer wishes to leave with the reader, then this method of telling a story is ideal.

Notice that in this example the person telling the story is *not* the main protagonist—unlike the narrator in a first person novel or story. This point is made at once as we see, not the narrator, but the protagonist, Jackie Shaw, coming toward us. The writer *must* decide from the first, however, just how active or passive an observer the narrator is going to be. Will he stay completely in the background, a disembodied voice, or will he be as active a participant in the story as was Nick Carraway in *The Great Gatsby?* Unless you make this decision early and stick to it, you will have great difficulty keeping your story in focus. Make no mistake about it, this is an exceedingly fine line to draw.

Objective Point of View

In the objective point of view, the writer shows his characters in action without going inside their minds. He stays strictly outside. His skill in objectively reporting the actions of his characters is what he relies on to indicate to the reader their motives and their emotional states as the story progresses.

An example:

Alec entered Sally's room. She did not look up, but continued her game of solitaire, the sound of the cards slapping down upon the card table the only sound in the stifling room save that of the lazily turning ceiling fan.

He closed the door, walked over and sat down on the musty cane sofa, and cleared his throat. She looked up at him then, a thin smile on her pale face.

"Get out of here," she said.

"Not right away."

"Yes. Right away."

"I've got to speak to you. About that business at the bar."

"I told you to get out." She picked up her cards with swift, angry swipes of her hand. Then she shot him a fierce glance. "Do you know how far a scream goes in this humidity?"

He got up quickly, his white suit already rumpled and damp from the closeness of the room. "All right. All right. But you'll tell me what I want to know. If not now, later."

"Get out!" she hissed.

He hurried from the room, closed the door behind him and stood there in the corridor for a moment, mopping his brow. Then he hurried off to the elevator.

Inside the room Sally shuffled her deck twice and began another game.

This is an extremely limiting viewpoint. What is in the mind of Alec? What is he thinking as he leaves the room? And Sally. What does she think and feel as Alec enters — and later, as he leaves? Of course, the reader can surmise much from what he has observed. But he is still only guessing.

These limitations seem arbitrary. The reader has the feeling that he is being restrained, held back from the conflict that he knows exists within the minds and hearts of the characters — and this conflict, after all, is something he has come to expect in fiction.

If this very tension, this suspense as to what is really motivating the characters is what the writer is after, he can employ this viewpoint to very great effect. It might be that what is going on in the minds of his people *must* be kept vague, that a precise rendering of their innermost reactions would reveal too much, would, in fact, anticipate the resolution.

Finally, there is a tightness, an economy in this point of view that has much to recommend it.

Assigned Point of View

The point of view that the beginning author should seriously consider is the assigned point of view.

It is called *assigned* because everything is told entirely from the lead character's viewpoint. Like the first person narrator, he is on stage at all times. Whatever happens in the story is filtered through his sensibilities. As a result we have most of the advantages that we have with the first person point of view.

But we do not have that one serious disadvantage discussed above. With this point of view we *can* view our main character from the outside. We can pull back from him, occasionally take a neutral stand, and just watch — in this way gaining some relief from his constant presence. Furthermore, with him no longer constantly yattering about himself, the maddening profusion of *I*'s will disappear.

Here's an example of the assigned point of view:

> The more Paul thought about it, the more uncertain he became. Of course, someone had to climb the wall and drop into the tall grass and high-tail it to Fort Victory, but why had Collier chosen him? What made Paul suddenly such a fast runner?
>
> Paul sat down on the stump, his long, youthful face drawn and white, his brow furrowed. What had just occurred to him seemed incredible; yet it was the only answer that made any sense at all.
>
> Mavis! he groaned to himself. Collier and Mavis! Of course!
>
> He got up quickly, snatched his rifle, and started back, his long, straw-colored hair billowing out behind him. He wasn't leaving now. He wasn't going anywhere. Not now, he wasn't. This better not be true, Mavis, he told himself, his knees weak with sudden rage. Not this time, Mavis — not with that skunk, Collier.

> He burst into the chart room without knocking. Collier was standing over the chart table with the General. Both men were obviously startled at the suddenness of his entry. Collier spun around to face Paul.
>
> "What is it? What happened?" he asked anxiously.
>
> "Is it the Indians?" the General asked. "Have they already begun the attack?"
>
> "No. It's not the Indians," Paul said, suddenly uncertain. Standing there, facing these two men, the rage that had galvanized him but a few seconds before vanished. His suspicions concerning Mavis and Collier appeared to him the delusions of a mad man.
>
> "I — I came to ask for more powder," he said.
>
> "Bursting in like that — for more powder?" Collier was plainly suspicious.
>
> "Well, give it to him, man," said the General. "He'll need it, most likely."

To give you a more accurate picture of the differences between this point of view and the first person viewpoint, let's rewrite that assigned point of view to make it first person:

> The more I thought about it, the more uncertain I became. Of course, someone had to climb the wall and drop into the grass and high-tail it to Fort Victory, but why had Collier chosen me? What made me suddenly such a fast runner?
>
> I sat down on the stump and tried to get this thing clear in my mind. What I came up with seemed incredible. Yet it was the only answer that made any sense at all.
>
> *Mavis!* I groaned to myself. *Collier and Mavis! Of course!*
>
> I got up quickly, snatched my rifle, and started back. I wasn't leaving now. I wasn't going anywhere. Not now, I wasn't. *This better not be true, Mavis,* I told myself, my knees weak with rage. *Not this time, Mavis—not with that skunk, Collier.*
>
>
> I burst into the chart room without knocking. Collier was standing over the chart table with the General. Both men were obviously startled at the suddenness of my entry. Collier spun around to face me.
>
> "What is it? What happened?" he asked anxiously.
>
> "Is it the Indians?" the General asked. "Have they already begun the attack?"
>
> "No. It's not the Indians," I said, suddenly uncertain. Standing there, facing these two men, the rage that had galvanized me but a few seconds before vanished. My suspicions concerning Mavis and Collier appeared to me to be the delusions of a mad man.
>
> "I—I came to ask for more powder," I said.
>
> "Bursting in like that—for more powder?" Collier was plainly suspicious.
>
> "Well, give it to him, man," said the General. "He'll need it, most likely."

Notice that in this first person version we gained intense identification with Paul. It was a lot easier to feel the anger he felt. But notice also that we had to omit valuable descriptive bits: *his long, youthful face drawn, his brow furrowed. . . . his long, straw-colored hair billowing out behind him.*

It may be that we would rather have the intensity and unity of the first person version even if we have to sacrifice that clearer picture of the protagonist we get when we see him in action from the outside. But there is no question that each point of view has advantages and disadvantages and that each must be weighed carefully before making a choice.

Yet if we decide we can dispense with the level of intensity and reader identification that a first person viewpoint offers, we will find that the assigned point of view also imparts a unity to the story, since—as mentioned earlier—whatever happens in the narrative is seen through the consciousness of the main character, giving us as unified a story line as we would have with the first person point of view. And reader identification, though not as intense as it is in first person, is still satisfactorily high.

Multiple Viewpoint

This viewpoint combines the advantages of the assigned point of view with that of the omniscient viewpoint. Since the omniscient point of view—as it used to be practiced—is no longer in favor, this refinement has developed in its stead. In most novels and stories today, in fact, the multiple viewpoint seems to be the most popular, by far.

Sticking with a single character—either by using the first person or assigned point of view—forces the writer, and thus the reader as well, to miss much of the action that must inevitably take place offstage with other characters. To force all the major action to take place within the purview of your single main character threatens believability not a little. The virtue of the multiple viewpoint is that it enables the writer to keep the reader where the action is without straining credulity.

Another good reason for using the multiple viewpoint is that with it the writer can deepen his or her characterization of many of the subsidiary characters. This is an especially valuable advantage when your story contains an adversary or villain in the old-fashioned sense. It is a fact that if those people moving against your protagonist are not adequately characterized, they will simply not seem as threatening—and your protagonist as threatened—as you would want. Consequently, your protagonist's eventual besting of his or her adversaries will not be seen as much of a triumph. Indeed, the more dimension you can give all of your major characters, the better your story will be—for remember, story is character in action.

The following excerpt illustrating the multiple point of view has had to be shortened for use in this text. But the advantages of this method should still be readily apparent.

. . . This time as Will rode back up through the rushing water, his eye watched the walls on both sides. In less than a mile he caught the slight fold of rock behind which a narrow trail could be glimpsed. He rode into it and soon found himself in a narrow canyon which allowed his horse passage only grudgingly. Presently he came out onto a grassy sward on a ledge overlooking the valley he had seen from above.

How many such hidden places as this there were in these mountains Will could only guess. But he was lucky to have found this one. Will took a quick look around. It was late in the afternoon, but he had plenty of sunlight left. He dismounted and began to lead his horse. Diego had not raised Will to take foolish chances—and riding into this valley aboard his black would be giving Weed Leeper a target too fat to miss.

As Will led the black down the narrow trail that wound deeper into the valley, Weed Leeper left the bank by the stream where he had been fishing that afternoon and started back through the pines toward his cabin. Returning with a string of four fat mountain perch, Weed was content.

It had been seven years since Weed had found this remote roost of his high in the Indian River Range. He had been forced to shoot his crippled mount and take refuge in a clump of pines outside the range, but he had been driven eventually up onto the ridge. It was later that same day, while looking for a dry campsite by the stream he had been forced to follow, that he had discovered the narrow canyon leading into this valley.

As he led his pack animal from the canyon and deeper into the valley, he had felt a profound awe at its incredible isolation and beauty. He realized at once that no other white man had ever explored these clear streams and the deep, fragrant woods, alive with the song of robins. When at last he came to the mountain lake and looked into its blue, clear depths, he knew he had found the perfect place: an Eden he could claim— and would claim—as his own.

From a filthy flat in St. Louis—where the vermin had free passage over the floors, the sink, the table, and even over his restlessly tossing body at night—Weed Leeper had fled west at the age of fifteen, certain that his widowed mother wouldn't care and filled with a desire for something better—and a black rage he made no effort to control. . . .

It wasn't long before his temper got him into a shooting, and before he was eighteen he had killed his first man. The brutal finality of his action had satisfied something deep within him, and soon he was riding with the Dawson Gang. . . .

But after finding his hidden valley, Weed discovered a purpose—to build in the valley and make it his own, away from the stench of humanity. And with a woman of his own, one he did not have to pay for each time.

Like Mary, Weed thought as he neared the cabin's entrance. She sure as hell protested when he took her, but at the same time she never took any opportunity to take after him with a knife or one of the guns. She liked it well enough, Weed had long since concluded. Besides, he'd suspect her if he found her sucking around him like some women he'd known. He liked his women to hate him just a little. He wouldn't have no respect for them otherwise.

Holding the string of perch away from his deerskin leggings, he leaned his sapling fishing pole against the side of the cabin and stepped into its cool interior.

Watching Weed approach the cabin across the clearing, Mary's fierce resolve almost deserted her. For more than two hours she had been waiting for his return— cursing him for his delay while at the same time praying that he would not come at all—that some blind stroke of fate would strike him down, ridding her of him forever. But of course it was not to be that simple, and that knowledge had overwhelmed her a moment before as she saw Leeper's lean frame emerge from the pines with the fresh, gleaming fish dangling from the line he held in his right hand.

But the moment of panic had passed, and she had tightened her grip on the large carving knife she had sharpened especially and then moved into the darkness beside the doorway, the knife brought up over her right shoulder. His footsteps were clearer now. She could smell the fish he was bringing. And then the doorway darkened as Weed's bulk filled it.

Hesitating only a moment, Weed stepped inside. Mary closed her eyes and brought the knife down in a furious, slashing arc. But he had caught her movement on the instant she left the wall and was turning when she struck, his right arm swinging up to ward off her blow. Mary felt the knife catch something; and at the same time her hand was struck and the knife sent flying from her hand.

Mary opened her eyes as Weed grabbed both her wrists and pulled her toward him. He had dropped the string of perch when he swung around, and struggling to pull away from Weed, her bare feet slipped on the fish and she lost her footing. As she fell Weed caught her up and with a snarl of pleasure strode with her across the floor to the mattress.

At once she realized his intentions and it drove her into a fury. She began beating upon him as she had done so often before. But as usual it did her little good. . . .

Weed made no effort to sit up, a delicious drowsiness falling over him. She was quiet now—her tears having long since given out. His left arm was bleeding steadily where she had stuck him. But he gave no thought to it.

What was that? He turned his head and looked out the open cabin doorway.

Weed blinked his eyes in a sudden effort to see more clearly. But even though he saw the man, he could not believe he was there. Will Caulder was approaching the doorway. He was less than a yard from it!

And in his right hand he held a Colt. . . .

Will had thought Weed was asleep. And stepping out of the sunlight into the cabin's cool dimness had given the edge to Weed. Before Will could see well enough to fire at Weed as he lay on the mattress, the man had sprung to his feet, dragging the woman upright as well. . . .

If the reader had been forced to remain with Will during his approach to the cabin, there would have been no apparent reason for Will being able to get so close to the cabin without detection. With the use of the multiple viewpoint, we not only know why Weed allowed Will to get so close before catching sight of him, but—despite the shortened versions of each segment—we also got very clear pictures of Mary and her abductor, Weed Leeper. Indeed, Mary emerges as a courageous but sorely pressed victim, while Weed is shown to be a thoroughly detestable sort.

Though some effort is made to give insight into Weed's motives and his personality, he is certainly a character whose utter ruthlessness will prove a real problem to Will, thus heightening the tension and the conflict. Remember what we said earlier: the more difficult and menacing the antagonist, the greater the conflict—and the excitement.

At the beginning of this discussion of point of view, it was pointed out that the single, restricted point of view— first person or assigned—gained for the writer both unity and reader identification. How then does one compensate for its loss when using this more diffuse viewpoint?

The writer simply accepts some dilution of effect in return for the sense of immediacy one achieves and for the depth in characterization that should result. It is a trade-off. Furthermore, the writer can do much to reduce this dilution of effect if he or she makes sure that whenever the viewpoint is shifted, what happens to this new individual is of vital concern to the lead and is a dramatic contribution to the forward momentum of the novel or story. Indeed, unless the shift accomplishes this, the change in viewpoint is unwise.

112

The multiple viewpoint, then, is an excellent way to broaden your characterization as well as to keep your reader on top of the action.

Omniscient Point of View

With this viewpoint the writer becomes a sort of ectoplasmic presence hovering over every character in the story, slipping in and out of first one mind and then another. God-like in his or her awareness, the writer knows all, sees all, and yet tells only that which in his judgment is best for the reader to know.

The problem with this viewpoint is that it can be quite a chore for the reader, since he is unable to settle back and identify with one character at a time—as in the multiple, assigned, or first person viewpoints. The reader must go scrambling along with the writer from one personality to another within the individual scenes without losing his bearings. Furthermore, with all this skipping around from person to person, the reader is constantly, naggingly aware of the author's incredible versatility. His apparent omniscience becomes, finally, a kind of intrusion.

Here's how it would go:

Bill Jackson looked across the jammed room at Glenda Roberts, who had just stepped out of a circle of animated guests. He lifted his glass to her and nodded, very slightly. The sudden gleam in her eye told him all he needed to know.

She has probably had another argument with Jim, he thought. *Poor Jim.*

Bill felt a surge of guilt at his part in all this, but he seemed helpless to take any other direction. It was as if Glenda had some kind of spell over him. *And she has,* he told himself in sudden dismay.

Glenda was watching Bill closely. When she saw him turn away abruptly, that pained look on his face, she realized at once what was bothering him. *His hand is in the cookie jar and he feels guilty,* she told herself scornfully. *Men!*

Jim, who had been watching his wife closely—even though he was apparently in active conversation with Martha Tilden—had caught at once the glance that passed between his wife and Bill Jackson. He had sensed as well the guilt Bill felt. *That won't cut any ice with Glenda,* he remarked to himself ironically as he smiled broadly back at Martha Tilden.

She had just told him that she had never missed a single one of his plays. It was an absurd claim, of course, but all he said was,

"Thank you, Martha. That's very flattering. But, you know, some of my plays, I realize now, were well worth missing."

She laughed, delighted. "You're so modest!"

She took his arm possessively and pulled him over to the divan, her sharp eyes devouring him. He tried to pull away without offending her, but couldn't seem to manage it. *He's not going down without a fight,* Martha noted grimly. *But he needs sympathy and understanding and he's going to get it.* She found nothing ingenuous in her attitude and would have been astonished if anyone were to think it so. She increased her grip on Jim's arm and smiled broadly as she pulled him down beside her on the sofa.

Glenda, watching Martha's progress, saw how frantically Jim was trying to disentangle himself, but she knew Martha well enough and glanced across at Bill, her gaze imperative. *Well, damnit,* she said to herself. *Get over here, Bill!*

Bill caught the look on Glenda's face and put his empty glass down on the table and started through the crush around it, his eyes on Glenda as she moved now lightly toward the French doors that opened onto the terrace. His pulse began to race, but he was sick at heart at the same time.

It was with enormous relief that he saw his wife leave the group she was entertaining and step toward him. He stopped to allow her to intercept him.

"Hi," he said. "Some party."

She smiled. "Yes, it is." She knew where he was going and felt a kind of icy coldness — not anger.

"Why don't we go home now?" she suggested abruptly.

"But . . . we just got here." Bill was astonished. Did she know? he wondered in a sudden panic. And then he realized that it didn't really make any difference. She was giving him an out.

"Yes," he told her, smiling suddenly. "Let's go home."

They said their goodbyes as every one remarked at their early departure; but Millie was the perfect hostess. She understood perfectly when she heard Lilian's polite excuse and thought to herself that here was a woman who might know how to handle Glenda. Now if she could keep her head about her. . . .

This was precisely what Lilian was doing as she sat beside Bill in the large quiet car and let him drive her home through the rain. As for Bill, he found himself thinking of Glenda back there at the party. He was just a little unhappy at the prospect of what this might mean to their relationship, and this apprehension caused him to frown slightly as he drove.

Noting Bill's silence and the frown, Lilian decided how she was going to make it clear to Bill that this was the end of his affair with Glenda without turning it into a big scene. She would simply tell Bill that she did not like the woman and would not go to any more parties where she was also in attendance. And she would see to it that Glenda was never again invited to her house. Bill would understand, she was sure. What Lilian hoped was that Bill had enough sense not to get gallant and try to defend Glenda, that he would simply shrug and let the matter drop. That should be sufficient, she told herself. Lilian had long since realized how much of a pushover Bill was for any designing female and had simply resolved to keep alert. But Glenda was considerably more than that. She took malicious pleasure in all the crockery she broke. Though Lilian hated to admit it to herself, she was now convinced that Glenda was what they called a predatory female.

Bill, aware suddenly of his wife's thoughtful silence, felt a slight unease. Again he asked himself if Lilian could possibly know about Glenda and him. He glanced quickly at Lilian. "A penny for your thoughts."

"Oh, they're worth more than that," she said, snuggling against his shoulder. . . .

Notice how the writer takes the reader from con- 115 sciousness to consciousness. We are inside the mind of one person and then almost before we can catch our breath, we find ourselves within another character, seeing the world from *that* vantage point. It can be a giddy experience.

This is what makes this viewpoint so different from the multiple viewpoint. In the latter case, as you will remember, once the writer has settled into a character, the reader remains locked inside that personality and remains there until the writer shifts his viewpoint again. Also, the writer is at great pains to alert the reader to each new shift. In that example of multiple viewpoint, you will recall how this was done: There was a four line transitional skip, the first sentence of the new viewpoint was not indented, and the pas-

sage began almost invariably with the name of the character
from whose consciousness the reader was expected to view
the action.

Obviously, no such care is taken in the omniscient
viewpoint. The result is a rather loosely constructed, pan-
oramic sweep that can be potentially interesting. Yet this
method tends to keep the readers at a distance. Possibly it is
the author's omniscient voice which causes this, becoming a
kind of barrier between the reader and the action.

What the omniscient viewpoint offers most of all, however, is that voice—that steady, understanding intelligence
that oversees the lives of its people like the shepherd his
flock. It can be a tragic universe, of course. Yet it is also a
tidy one. Intrusive though the narrator's voice might be, it
can have its charm. And, of course, as in the above example,
that voice can be very effectively muted.

If you decide on this viewpoint, be sure your omniscient
voice is muted as well.

Author Intrusion

The intrusion I have been discussing in the omniscient viewpoint is a much more subtle, less offensive kind of intrusion—the voice of the narrator:

> *She found nothing ingenuous in her attitude and
> would have been astonished if anyone were to think it
> so.*

> *They said their goodbyes as everyone remarked at
> their early departure; but Millie was the perfect hostess.
> She understood completely when she heard. . . .*

> *This was precisely what Lilian was doing as she sat
> beside Bill in the large quiet car and let him drive her
> home through the rain. . . .*

This intrusion can get out of hand, of course, but the
kind of intrusion that is always out of hand is that which
might better be labeled Author's Big Mouth.

In other words, how would you like it if every once in a
while the director or the writer of the film you were watching were to hop up onto the stage and warn you of complications yet to come? You wouldn't like it. You would be

reminded that what you were seeing had not really taken place and was actually a product fabricated for an evening's entertainment. Any illusion of reality would have been shattered completely:

> Peter strode purposefully down the side street, determined to have it out with Sam Ruggles once and for all. *However, as events would soon prove, he would have been a lot wiser if he had let this quarrel with Sam pass; but Peter, as we saw earlier, was an impetuous youth unwilling to recognize the folly of a quick temper.*
>
> Peter stormed into the bar . . .

The italicized sentence in that example is the intrusion. There used to be a time when an author could do this. In fact, it was expected of him. But that day is long past. Today the author is expected to tell his story and let the reader draw his own conclusions—or at least appear to do so. For naturally, the writer has total control over the events and the characters in his story. They are the creatures of his imagination. With this in mind, it is obvious that any conclusions the reader draws will be pretty much those conclusions the writer wants him to draw. But even so, this must happen without the writer stepping into the narrative and telling the reader how to view the actions of his characters. Certainly it is uncalled for when the writer gives away a plot complication because he simply can't keep his mouth shut.

This intrusion is more likely to occur in the frame within a frame point of view, since with this viewpoint, the observer-narrator is constantly commenting on the action and the main character. But it can happen with other viewpoints—especially the omniscient view—and the writer should be constantly on his guard against this kind of author intrusion.

In summary, of all the vantage points from which a story can be told, each one has advantages unique to it. The writer must decide which viewpoint is best for his particular story, weighing the advantages and disadvantages carefully before coming to a decision. And no matter which viewpoint is chosen, the author must remember to keep off the stage. It is his people and their story alone that matter.

Let's Experiment Some With Viewpoints

1. Write a long scene—again taking the sequence from that plot treatment you wrote earlier—using first person. Then rewrite the whole scene again, this time using the assigned point of view.

2. Write the same scene in objective point of view.

3. Choose four other characters from that notebook—or create four "new" people—and dramatize them, using the multiple point of view, moving from character to character throughout the scene or chapter.

4. Write a short slice-of-life vignette about a down-and-out ballplayer or musician, or an old soldier—any character along these lines, using the frame within a frame point of view, with the observer taking some minor part in the vignette. What you want here is a framed character-sketch, with the frame only the voice of the observer, who at the end tries to sum up what the condition of these people means.

chapter eleven

Theme

"Have something to say, and say it as clearly as you can. That is the only secret."

MATTHEW ARNOLD

"To have something to say is a question of sleepless nights and worry and endless ratiocination of a subject — of endless trying to dig out of the essential truth, the essential justice."

F. SCOTT FITZGERALD

In this chapter you will find theme considered as a statement that should guide you in your selection and rejection of those characters and events that make up the *body of your story or novel. You should finally be able to find and formulate the theme statement for your own work of fiction.*

Characters First, Then Theme

You should seldom if ever start your novel or short story with a specific theme in mind. It just won't work very well. Instead, you should start with characters who demand to be given whatever life you can create for them on the printed page. It is the characters who must galvanize you to write, insisting that you tell their story.

But you can never really know your characters' full story until you begin to write about them. So you begin to write. But after a promising start, however, you find yourself struggling as your characters seem to take a kind of malicious delight in leading you astray. You may find at last that you have bogged down completely. You don't seem to be getting anywhere and your characters — now that they have worn you out — are fast asleep.

This may sound like a flippant way to describe a serious problem — one that many writers experience at one time or another — but essentially, this is what seems to happen.

What is wrong? The answer — in many cases — is that you, the writer, do not know what it is your characters are trying to say, what their story means. In other words, though you seldom if ever should start with a theme, you must eventually find a theme in the process of writing.

Finding Your Theme

Obviously, then, it is characters who come first and it is from them that you will get your theme. Ask yourself what it is that intrigues you about the characters you have selected. Who is the most interesting person? And why? What does that character represent to you? Perhaps your theme lies in those answers.

Another solution is to go back over what you have already written. Often you will find your theme buried back there in a statement by one of your main characters. It had been there all the time, waiting for you to come back for it.

And then let us say you have found a theme that galvanizes you once more, gives life, purpose, and direction to your narrative—until you find all of a sudden that you no longer agree with the statement your story or novel is making. Another theme has insinuated itself into your narrative. Perhaps a different character is emerging, or is actually beginning to take over—and you find yourself on his or her side.

And this might necessitate a change of theme.

All right then. Stop. Read over what you have written. Then make your decision. Either eliminate this character and go on from there the way you had been going—or give up and join forces with this other character. Change the rest of your story in accordance with your new theme and go on.

Often the different theme is really only a variation on the original one. Yet it may be an important variation—usually a twist of some kind. What often happens is that you find you have really very little revision when you adapt to this new theme, since this was the direction in which you had been heading all along.

Theme as Statement

Think of *theme* as a single statement, that is, a sentence complete with a subject and a predicate. Not a single word. Nor a few words like: *The unhappiness that comes with the end of summer.* That is not a sentence and therefore not a statement.

It is crucial that you understand the difference between a sentence and a few words that might sound impressive, but be worth absolutely nothing as a theme. Let's take that sentence fragment I quoted earlier—*The unhappiness that comes with the end of summer*—and examine it closely.

Such a fragment at first appears to have all kinds of significance. But has it? What does it actually say? For a poem this fragment might be enough, but not for a story. What about that unhappiness? What conclusion should be drawn concerning it? What is missing here is the verb. So we turn this fragment into a complete sentence:

The unhappiness that comes with the end of summer is inevitable, since like the seasons, everything changes—happiness to unhappiness, joy to sorrow, love to hate.

Of course, when we try to encapsulate any story or novel into a single theme statement, we find that we reduce it more often than not to a somewhat banal bromide that excites only our condescension. But we should remember that it is not this banality the writer is presenting to his reader as much as his unique, perhaps ironic, treatment of it.

Theme as an Aid in Revision

It does not matter how banal the theme might seem to the writer. When the writer is working on his story, he needs this statement to keep him on the right track; for unless he realizes the importance of having a theme to clothe as he writes, he is apt to cut, slash, and revise endlessly, purposelessly — all to no avail. In the end he may never know when he is finished, and then he can only abandon his manuscript and try something else.

On the other hand, with a sense of what his theme is, the writer will find that he needs to do much less revision, and that what revision he does will be done with relative speed and lack of hesitation. Since this scene or that character is not really needed to bolster the theme, out it goes. And that is that.

This ability to revise intelligently is a very great advantage and — more than any other single factor — is what separates the professional writer from the amateur.

Is Theme the Moral?

No. When you point a moral, you are giving a piece of advice; telling someone what to do. A theme, on the other hand, is simply a statement about human beings or about life in general. In fact, the last thing you will want to do is start preaching. Nothing offends readers today more than the realization that they are being lectured to, told what to do. It is this fact, indeed, that is at the root of most parent–child conflict. So don't become a parent–writer lecturing your child–reader. One of the best ways to guard against making this mistake is to be sure that your theme is not a didactic assertion concerning the rightness or wrongness of any particular line of personal conduct.

Is Theme Propaganda?

Doesn't knowing what your theme is mean you will end up writing message novels or propaganda? Of course not. But think a moment. No one speaks to another person without some purpose in mind — however feebly this point might be articulated. Otherwise, why speak at all? Every well thought out utterance between people — in order to be valid — must make an intelligent statement.

And so should your story or novel.

The Nature of Your Theme

In my first published novel the theme was simple enough: Major league baseball is a business; but it is also a game.

In Hammett's *The Maltese Falcon* the hero commits himself to finding his partner's killer, despite the fact that he had hated his partner. He does this because his partner was his partner. Though it develops that the hero has to turn in someone he has come to love, he does it anyway. A partner is a partner. It is this code of honor, necessary for survival in the world the private detective inhabits, that is Hammett's theme, giving point and bite to every scene in the book. Nothing very profound in Hammett's theme, of course, but as pointed out earlier, it is what is done with a theme that matters.

The point to all this is that while writing a story or novel, the writer must have some theme to aid in the selection and rejection of each character, scene, and plot development. Though the writer may have difficulty finding the correct theme and though it may change in midstream, without one, the writer will find that no unified story is possible. Finally, without a theme the writing will be brutally difficult, with each session at the typewriter a trial; with a theme clearly in mind, however, the writing will go almost 123 famously.

Or at least as well as a writer deserves.

Now To Find Your Theme

1. For some time now you have been working on a plot treatment based on one or two of your notebook characters. Now begin to study that treatment very carefully and see if you can discern the theme of the plot. If you can, reduce it to a statement — and do not shudder too much when you discover that it does not contain the wisdom of the ages.

2. If you cannot find a theme in your treatment, study some of the other characters in the notebook. What themes do their lives suggest to you? Write as many out as you can. Select the one that interests you and write a treatment exemplifying that theme.

3. If not a single character in your notebook is capable of inspiring a theme, invent a character out of the blue and begin writing about this person until you discern the germ of a theme emerging.

part three

THE ACT OF WRITING

For the remainder of this book, we will assume that you are working on your own short story or novel, deriving, I hope, encouragement and the necessary expertise from each chapter as you go. Think of the author of this text as a writer acquaintance of yours sitting across the kitchen table from you, two steaming cups of black coffee between us as we work together on this story or novel you are writing.

chapter twelve

Inspiration or Perspiration

"To be a writer is to sit down at one's desk in the chill
portion of every day, and to write; not waiting for the
little jet of the blue flame of genius to start from the
breastbone—just plain going at it, in pain and delight. To
be a writer is to throw away a great deal, not to be
satisfied, to type again, and then again, and once more,
and over and over . . ."

JOHN HERSEY

*In few other fields of human endeavor is the
psychological factor as critical as it is in the writing of
fiction. This confrontation with oneself can be a terrifying
experience when the aspiring writer decides he no longer*

wishes to consider himself an amateur. All of a sudden it is for real. You should gain comfort from this chapter then, as you see how typical are those personal reactions you have been agonizing over for so long in solitude.

Ready for the Icy Plunge

You are on the edge of the cliff, ready to make that dive into the icy waters far below. But it is night, and you are not so sure you want to try it. Not tonight. Some other night perhaps — but not tonight.

That Blank Page

That's how it feels to face that clean white sheet of paper. It all seemed so simple and uncomplicated until you came to this moment. Now your mind is a white blank, a mirror image of that piece of paper staring back at you from the typewriter. You begin to sweat; you get up for a cigarette, a cup of coffee, both — and hope the telephone will ring.

You've got writer's palsy, something all writers get when confronted with that terrifyingly empty page. It is perfectly normal, a disability you will have to get used to. Just don't give in to it. Grit your teeth and sit at the typewriter and *force* yourself to write.

At times I have just bowed my head forward and rested it on the deck of my typewriter and slowly, deliberately typed first one word, then another and another until the sentences began to flow. This is an extreme example, but this *is* the way it is at times.

128

Why bring this up now? Because you are likely to find yourself in this kind of a bind when you first sit down to write. What I am saying is *PERSIST*. If you have to, sit and stare at the paper until you begin to write. The solution is really that simple. Whenever you think you are not writing well enough to go on, just keep going until at last, the dam bursts.

The Capricious Guest

"What about inspiration?" you ask. Forget it. How many times have I heard young — and old — would-be writers tell me that they never wrote until they felt inspired—"in the proper mood" was usually the way they expressed it. Of course, the truth is they never write—not for publication, that is. They simply haven't the willingness to bleed.

Does this mean that writers are never inspired, never write in a fever of enthusiasm as they clamber after that wild goat to the pinnacle? Of course not. It means only that inspiration comes if you do not wait for it. Inspiration—so-called—comes more often than not *after* you have started to write (if it is going to come at all).

Tchaikovsky referred to inspiration as the Capricious Guest who refused to visit the lazy, but who came when you were quite busy. He was quite right. But when this guest does arrive, you will find your fingers fairly flying over the keys. It is an astonishing experience. Delightful twists in the plot, solutions to nagging technical problems, sudden insights into your characters all seem to have come with such ease and are so right that you find it difficult to believe you had anything at all to do with the performance. As a result of these experiences, your humility, when you are asked to accept credit for what you have done, is genuine. It really seems as if that Capricious Guest had done it all. You were just the medium through which his genius flowed—the observer, almost, as he performed.

As I said, you cannot wait for him to arrive. You must proceed as if you were never going to experience his help again. In fact, it almost seems as if you must reach a point at which you do not need him before he will step into your room and sit down with you at the typewriter.

Thus it is often that you write alone, without the aid of that guest. Keep on writing, nevertheless. If you do, you will discover a curious thing: When you look back at the prose you created while you were slogging it out and compare this writing with that which you wrote supposedly under full flush of "inspiration," you will most likely find little discernible difference in quality between the two.

With that in mind, keep on. Write at a steady pace without looking back. You'll do fine during some stretches and poorly during others. Never mind. Yet that does *not* mean you should ever write sloppily. Write carefully and as well as you know how, always, but stay at your desk. If you start slowing down or going back to read over what you have written, if you start debating over the choice of a word, you are heading for trouble. Something within you is trying to stop you, and this is the best way to do so, by getting you overly finicky.

Later you will rewrite, but not now.

The Daily Schedule

You can't do it all in one day. You'd like to be able to do so, of course, but that's out of the question. You do it a page at a time, slowly, steadily, rain or shine—every day.

This means you must have a writing schedule, a time and a place each day where you will go and write your two or three pages.

"Only two or three?" you say. Is that enough? Of course it is, at first. For one thing, too large a goal every day, such as five or ten pages—that's almost two thousand words— might work for a while, but it would eventually become a considerable strain, and you would soon find yourself dreading the daily stint and manufacturing perfectly plausible reasons for not going to your desk. On the other hand, if your daily page total is relatively small, you will often find yourself writing more than you planned.

When this happens, a very good idea is to cut the next day's total. If you have a daily four-page goal, say, and one day you do five or even six pages, the next day you should feel perfectly satisfied to write only two or three pages.

Then there will be times when your wife or husband and the children will want to go somewhere for the weekend. The solution is easy enough. Just steam ahead of your modest daily page total for three or four days until you have reached the total number of pages you would have written had you worked through the weekend. Then take off on that trip and relax, secure in the knowledge that your page total is not suffering one bit as a result of this weekend away from your desk. It will make quite a difference to your state of mind.

Getting the Writing Habit

Once you begin to write in this fashion, you will find it gives you immense satisfaction. You will develop a self-discipline toward your writing you had probably never developed toward anything else in your life. It will become a habit, and you will find yourself feeling guilty whenever you fail to complete your projected daily page total. All the while, the pile of pages containing your story or novel will get heftier and heftier, like a promise coming closer.

How to Keep Going

There is an excellent device you may use for writing at a nice clip without interrupting the flow to put new sheets of paper into the typewriter. Scotch tape your pages together, fifteen or so pages at a stretch, and then keep writing until you run out. You'll have to experiment to get the pages taped together correctly so the paper will continue on through the typewriter.

You need only small squares of Scotch tape at the upper left and upper right hand corners to hold the pages together, making sure that one edge overlaps the other. When you finish the fifteen or so pages, a razor will cut through the tape. You'll be surprised at how this aids the flow.

When you do stop writing for the day, try *not* to stop at the end of a major incident or chapter. Do everything you can to stop *during* something exciting — in the middle of a sentence if you can manage it. The rule is simple: Stop while the juices are still flowing, for if you wait until they have dried up, when you feel emptied or drained, there is going to be some difficulty in getting yourself back on the track the next day.

When you have trouble getting started, even with this trick, read over what you have already written. Assuming you know what *should* happen next, retype the last few paragraphs or even pages. When you come to where you left off the day before, keep right on going, as if there were never any doubt at all as to how you were going to proceed.

131

Writer's Block

Let us assume that in spite of all these dodges, you are straining mightily, but can bring forth nothing larger than a few beads of perspiration. All right then. Regard this as a warning that something is wrong with your plot complication at this juncture. Perhaps the characterization of your lead is awry. Something within you is telling you that something fundamental is wrong, and that is why you can't proceed.

The trouble is that you don't know what is wrong. All you have at this point is that real inability to get going again. You will just have to ride it out as best you can. Go over the pages you have typed already. Put them in the same notebook as the outline we will discuss later and carry the notebook around with you everywhere you go. You'll be astonished at how many times in the course of the day you'll get a few minutes free to go over what you have written.

As you read over the pages, ink corrections in the margins or on the other side of the pages; or insert new pages with freshly written sections on them. Glance over the outline, too, reading snatches of it here and there. Ponder it. Ponder the theme. Get to the point where this whole project is gnawing at a corner of your mind from the moment you get up in the morning until you go to sleep at night.

Since during all this time you will not be moving ahead on your story or novel, you will get panicky. Two, perhaps three days have gone by and still you have written nothing new. Are you written out? Could it be that this whole project is insane, that you're just a madman playing Caesar? . . . Then one evening you sit down and begin to write, and the solution comes to you. That Capricious Guest, perhaps. At any rate, suddenly you *know* what's wrong, what needs to be changed. At once the way is clear again.

Note that I said the solution comes *after* you sit down and *begin to write*. You *must* dip the oar in yourself and begin to pull — hard — or nothing will happen. Your subconscious simply will not work for you unless you do your share as well.

What you will probably find after you are under way again is that you will have to make some important adjustments in your characterizations and in your plot. Don't complain. Be grateful. It is far better to make these changes now in the process of writing than later after the pages have been completed, the scenes all written, the characters fully realized.

132

In summary, the secret of inspiration is work. That's really all there is to it. Nothing very profound about that. Keep writing at a steady clip, holding to a modest daily total of pages. When you hit a snag, stay at it and worry — like a dog his bone — your outline and what you have already written until the break comes and you can move on. What you must have is faith — faith that if you keep going, if you keep pondering your story and your people, it will all turn out well, faith that your Capricious Guest will appreciate the effort you are making and will help to pull you through.

Remember, you must keep working.

Now That You Are About to Begin Work on Your Story or Novel

Discuss in class the following points made in this chapter:

1. You must be able to slog on without waiting for inspiration.
2. You must establish a modest production schedule, and keep to it.
3. You should stop writing every day at a point from which you are really eager to go on — in other words, while the juices are still flowing.
4. You must have faith in yourself as a writer.

chapter thirteen
Openings

"Get it down. Take chances. It may be bad, but it's the
only way you can do anything really good."
WILLIAM FAULKNER

Getting started is difficult, since you find you have
embarked on a journey so filled with hidden turnings and
blind alleys that it intimidates from the very beginning.
What you will learn in this chapter is how formal — and
therefore comparatively simple — your opening pages can be.

The basic pattern for openings is the same for the short story as it is for the novel. Sketch in the locale, put your lead character on stage quickly, and see to it that the problem and the theme are hinted at if not openly presented.

Let's try an opening to see how it goes:

> The moisture-laden clouds hung oppressively over Greenwich. Fans droned futilely. Air conditioners labored helplessly, seemingly unable to banish the mugginess. It had rained a little while ago, around three, but it was a fitful, useless rain that only seemed to transform the suburb into a vast Turkish bath.
>
> Pete Brewster deftly pulled his Chevy up to the curb across the street from a white house sitting back on a neat, well-manicured lawn. He slammed out of the car, hurried across the street and up the walk to the white house. Despite the heat, he looked as cool as a Tom Collins in green-striped pants, tight at the waist, narrow at the ankle, a yellow short-sleeved shirt. His shiny black hair was cut off raggedly just above the collar.
>
> Whistling, he pressed the button. Almost at once the door was pulled open and Janet stood in the doorway, a quick smile lighting her face.
>
> "Surprised, Chicken?"
>
> "Come in!" she cried, pulling him in and closing the door, her eyes wide with surprise. They were almond-shaped, large and brown, luminous now with excitement. "Of course I'm surprised. Why didn't you call?"
>
> He looked quickly around the waxed, immaculate living room and dining area. Then he looked back at her with a wide grin. "Where's Ed?"
>
> "You know where he is," she said, smiling. She was standing close to him again, waiting. He could feel her waiting. He thought he'd prolong it for just a moment — one more delicious moment.
>
> "The wife's gone," he said. "To Columbus. Something about a sick sister. She'll be gone for a week."
>
> With a squeal of delight she was in his arms, her lips . . .

These two people are obviously having an affair. They

may be nice people, or they may not be so nice. But no matter, they are heading for trouble. And the reader will want to read on to see what happens to them.

After this opening you might plan something that would precipitate a crisis in this couple's relationship. It may even develop that the girl has decided to confess her affair to her husband, and ask him for a divorce, thus freeing her to marry our hero. Of course, she expects her lover to greet this announcement with pleasure and tell her that he intends to divorce *his* wife so that he can marry her. But he intends to do no such thing, and an argument develops.

It is still going on when a car pulls into the drive. Ed is back unexpectedly. The two lovers quickly patch over their quarrel, and this opening scene ends with the protagonist making a hasty exit and driving off:

> He was out the kitchen door in an instant. Flattening himself against the rear wall of the garage, he waited until he heard the car door slam, then the squeak of the screen door before he stepped over the low fence to the driveway next door. Sauntering casually to the sidewalk, he crossed the street to his car and drove off without a backward glance.
>
> He was pleased, thinking of how smoothly he had left and how Janet had clung to him until the very last minute. She was gone on him, all right. And she was all woman. Every bit. Every little bit.
>
> He braked for a red light and drummed impatiently on the steering wheel as a nasty shard of a thought broke into his pleasant mood. Janet still had this crazy idea that he wanted to divorce Clara and marry her.
>
> The light changed. In a squeal of rubber he was off, beating a black Cadillac to the next corner and cutting it off. . . .

Perhaps you noticed that what we have here is a hint of what complications are going to develop. This was done by showing the thoughts of the main character—an excellent way to close a scene with suspense. A man's thoughts can be as violent and as tension-provoking as his actions. Note also, as this opening scene closes, how the protagonist's thoughts and the way in which he drives characterize him.

Let's review now. The opening description of the weather and the locale served to set the tone and establish the writer's style, while it gave the necessary background for the action. Since it is a hot, sultry day, we have an atmospheric condition ideally suited for the kind of tension and conflict this story is about to dramatize. A softer, more bucolic setting would have indicated a totally different kind of story.

The problem is introduced early. We soon learn that this is not going to be a novel dealing with campus unrest, nor is it science fiction. There is plenty of movement, and we are introduced to our characters quickly. We know who and what they are, and certainly we know their problems.

Don't Bore the Reader

You must not open too slowly. There's a lot you have to do, and you don't have much time in which to do it. You must do it and do it without boring your reader, for it is in the opening pages that you must grab your reader and keep him. You will have no other chance.

Don't fuss about this obligation you have to your reader, since you don't really have much choice. After all, you are competing with the football game on TV, the local movie house, concerts, stereo. In addition, the writer's potential reader must, for the sake of reading his work, be willing to isolate himself from his family and friends in order to give his full attention to what the writer has created. Not only that, he will usually have to pay for the privilege.

So that opening had better be good.

138   After that Fast Start, Ease Off

Your opening scene is done. Now you can take your foot off the accelerator and slow down some. In your next few scenes give your reader some time to get comfortable, to find out more about the locale, the minor characters, and more, much more, about your leads. Watch the next good motion picture and notice how, after the first splurge of attention-grabbing action, the pace slows, and you settle into a nice introductory scene that immediately begins to characterize the leads still more.

It is standard operating procedure. Now let's go back to our philanderer and see how this easing-off process might work:

Pete closed the door and walked lazily, contentedly across the large, air-conditioned living room, his footfalls soundless on the deep pile wall-to-wall carpet Clara had just had installed. He chuckled to himself at the old dame's reason for replacing the carpet. Too many cigarette holes in it, she'd said. There had been only two and both of them were nearly invisible to the naked eye. Yessir, one thing about Clara. She was no cheapskate.

He pushed aside the sliding glass doors and stepped out onto the terrace and looked down at the world. All he saw were the tops of trees, a patch of the drive, and the mountains of western Connecticut in the distance. At this height the air was almost cool.

He went back inside, built himself a Scotch on the rocks, and slumped down on the sofa, kicking off his light, fifty-nine sixty shoes as he did so. A panel on the arm of the sofa activated the color TV. He tried a few channels, turned off the set in annoyance, and scratched under his left arm.

He was bored. He reached past the panel for the phone and dialed a number. Leaning back, he smiled as he heard the voice on the other end.

"Marsha. How are you, girl? This is Pete. Just got back in town. I wondered if you might still remember me."

He laughed and sat up. She remembered him, all right.

"That's right. I'm the guy with the penthouse and the stereo. Was there something else you remembered about me?"

139

He laughed.

"Okay. Okay. That's me, all right. Say, I was thinking. How about you and I. . . ."

This scene is slow, but it certainly gives a picture of Pete Brewster's life style as the husband of Clara. And certainly Brewster's call to Marsha leaves no doubt in the reader's mind as to how seriously this fellow is taking his affair with Janet. And obviously he is very comfortable in this penthouse. It is most unlikely that Pete Brewster will give all this up to marry a suburban housewife, no matter how sexy she might be.

Of course Janet does not yet realize this.
The story is now underway.

To summarize, then, we find that after a fast opening, it is best to slow the pace to allow for a more leisurely introduction of the locale and the characters. But at no time do we waste time or dawdle.

And Now to Get Going on that Book or Story

Write your opening scenes or chapter and bring them into the class and read them aloud to your fellow students. It would be a good idea to have them listen for the following points:

1. Do we know the names of the main characters soon enough? Are the characters who are introduced well enough differentiated, so that we are not confused as to who is who?

2. Do we know the time of day, the locale, the season—if these are pertinent to setting the mood?

3. How soon do we know the main protagonist's problem? We should know from the very beginning why this is *his* story. It need not be stated baldly, but it should be hinted at, certainly implied.

4. After the opening sequence or scene, which should certainly grab and sustain the reader's interest, do we have a slower, more leisurely pace during which we learn still more concerning our protagonist and his problem?

When you write an opening scene for a short story or the opening chapter or chapters of a novel, I hope that you will keep the above-mentioned points in mind as you write—and also that a theme will occur to you as you work—for from that will come the outline you will need if this beginning is to amount to anything.

Meanwhile, don't forget: A plot is a person in some kind of a bind.

chapter fourteen

Making an Outline

Now that you have begun your opening scenes or chapters and have a reasonably clear picture of your characters, it is time for you to hold back and consider your outline. At the conclusion of this chapter, you should be able to start your own. And don't get edgy. You'll finish that story or novel soon enough. Patience.

An outline should be thought of as a rough treatment of your story or novel, something tangible you can refer to when the going gets difficult. Think of it as a good deal more detailed than those plot treatments you have been using up until now. If you are restless at the thought of an outline, remember that when you do not know what you are trying to say or how you are going to say it, there is not much likelihood you will perform very brilliantly, whether it be a short story or a novel. Sinclair Lewis's outline for *Arrowsmith* ran to 60,000 words; and Arthur Hailey's outlines usually take up to six months to complete, and each is rewritten three to four times before Hailey considers it ready to be used as a map for that long journey ahead, as he calls it.

Opening to Outline

For me, the first item of business used to be working out a theme statement, and from that, working out my outline. It was devilishly difficult work, and often I had to rewrite extensively when I discovered the theme I had started with was not what I wanted after all. But since I had published close to thirty teenage sports novels and mysteries using this method, I was reluctant to switch to another. Since turning to adult category fiction, however, I have found myself working faster and enjoying it more by writing out my opening chapters first—actually getting acquainted with my characters—and then settling down to the task of delineating my theme, and from that, fashioning an outline.

It is still no easy task to sweat out that outline, but it does seem to come a lot faster now—and I seldom have to revise it as often as before. Let's see how it works.

As I said, I start to ponder my outline after my opening chapter or chapters are completed. That is, they are written as well as I know how, though I realize that revisions will most likely be required later. I have selected from that notebook—or from that backroom in the corner of my mind—my lead characters, and have put them on stage as described in the preceding chapter. My protagonist is in difficulty and the outlook is not good. The locale has been described and I have a dim idea of what is to follow.

But only a dim idea. By this time, I am usually in a constant sweat as I try to figure out what is going to happen next—or if what I know is going to happen next should happen. As you can see, it is time for me to work out my outline.

The first step is selecting my theme statement. I read over the opening chapters, imagine the rest of the story—and try to give the book a title. If I cannot give it a reasonable working title, I realize I do not yet have a theme. I stick to the task until I find either the title or the theme. And I do this with the knowledge that both title and theme may be long gone before the book is done.

Finally, I have the theme statement or title, whichever says it best. No matter how banal it may sound, I accept it and proceed from there to step two, the writing of the synopsis.

I don't go into any great detail at this stage. All that is needed here is a brief, running account of the bones of the story. I keep this synopsis as short as possible, about two or three pages long.

Now you have a quick, convenient overview of your entire story or novel. It's all there. And all that is needed at this point is development in the form of an outline. And that's step number two.

Here's the beginning of a synopsis for one of my earlier novels:

> Bob and Jeff are swimming in Pirate Cove late one evening. Getting back into his boat, Jeff glances across the cove and sees what appears to be a sea serpent. He and his friend investigate the sighting, then leave for home. While driving parallel to the cove, they see it again, but only for an instant. Then Jeff tries to borrow a motor boat to investigate, but his request is refused, and he goes on home with Bob, who is staying with him.
>
> The next day he is no longer so sure he saw anything. After all, a sea serpent! His father also kids him. He decides to forget it, Jeff too. The boys go skin diving in the cove and meet Jane Parkhurst—Girl friend?—and she tells them she saw the serpent too!

The synopsis went on like that for two full pages, relating in broad outline how the community proceeded to take advantage of the tourists from all over who flocked to Pirate Cove for a look see at a real serpent, and what happened when the boys discovered the serpent was a fake.

The third and final step was the actual construction of the outline. I went over the synopsis and divided it roughly into chapters. When you try this, you will just have to feel your way. Usually, chapter breaks come where there is a falling off of incident, a climax of some kind, or a lapse in time.

In the synopsis above, I decided on a new chapter after Jeff was refused the motorboat. This allowed me to begin the second chapter with the next day. It seemed a natural place for a break.

Once you have made your chapter divisions, go along as I did: Take out a fresh sheet of paper and type at the head of it the number of the chapter. Then copy onto the sheet what you have down in your synopsis for that chapter. As you do so, allow yourself to elaborate on the synopsis. Add in those details, scraps of dialogue, bits of business that will later be used to bring this chapter to life.

Do not go overboard here, but if a witty crack should occur to you, put it down; or if the fragment of a particularly well-imagined scene should present itself — possibly a scene crucial to an understanding or working out of a character's motivation or of an understanding of the theme — do not hesitate to include it also.

Now comes a very important step. Try to divide each chapter into at least three separate scenes as you type up the chapter material. This may seem arbitrary at first, but you'll be surprised at how it will aid in your invention, and help the chapter to move along. The longer your chapter, of course, the more scenes you should think in terms of; but three to four scenes — on an average — is a nice goal to shoot at. Do this and you'll be granted a fine bonus: You'll have yourself thinking of your story in terms of scenes, something that is very important.

When you have finished transferring your synopsis to the chapter pages, you will have as many pages as you have chapters, with a rough idea on each as to what will happen in that particular chapter, scene by scene. By this time you will have noticed that your original synopsis has expanded considerably.

This, then, is your outline.

Enter the Subconscious

The act of typing up the outline should put your subconscious to work on the book as a whole. (You got some hint of this process when you typed up each chapter from the synopsis.)

Now, as you go about your usual business, ideas relative to your novel will start occurring to you. You'll find yourself picking out isolated scraps of information from newspapers and magazines you would not have noticed before – and doing this because they fit somewhere in your novel. For example, my novel, *The Serpent of Pirate Cove*, involved two young boys who were skin divers. As I worked on the outline and the opening chapters of the book, I began noticing references to skin diving on all sides, coming at me from all directions, it seemed. Of course, this information had been there all along. I had simply turned it off, since I did not need it. But now I needed it. The subconscious knew this and turned on the switch. The flood was on.

Handling the Flood

How do you take advantage of this subconscious flow? Buy one of those three-hole punches. Then get hold of a loose-leaf notebook and punch holes in those chapter sheets you typed and place them in the notebook. Now fill up each chapter page with anything more you come up with and re-insert the page into the notebook. When you run out of space for the new material constantly occurring to you, simply type it up on another page, punch holes in it also, and place it with the proper chapter heading in the notebook.

What you will then have is a loose-leaf notebook containing your chapter outline, an outline that will slowly grow over the weeks and months as you add more and more material. Suppose, for instance, that somewhere in your novel your characters are going to get caught in a sudden shower and take refuge in a gazebo. For some screwy reason you want this quaint and homely structure to shelter them from the rain, and you have this particular bit of business scheduled to take place somewhere in the tenth chapter.

You are out walking one evening, turn a corner, and there's a broken down old house. In the back of it you see a decaying gazebo, the white paint peeling from its slats and posts. You hurry into the back yard and look it over carefully; you stamp around inside it; you inspect every nook and cranny – and with its image fresh in your mind, you hurry home to write down on a sheet of paper what you remember of the gazebo, punch holes in the paper, and insert it in the notebook with all of the other material you have collected for chapter ten.

When you finally get to the tenth chapter, there will be this fresh, vivid description, just right for getting you started again.

Revising the Outline

As you continue to build your outline, keep that theme of yours always in mind. Every once in a while, stop and reread the outline to make sure that it properly dramatizes that statement you settled on.

If it doesn't, you'd better seriously consider the possibility of revising the outline, for here in your outline is where your major revisions should take place. A good outline is one that you can revise, or at least one that will make later revisions minor and easily handled.

When you are confronted with wholesale revisions, when you find you must discard whole chapters, radically change or delete complete characters, you have only your outline to blame. Revisions of such magnitude should have been considered while you worked over your outline as you carried it around with you, adding and deleting, imagining this scene or that, including details, notes on locale, and so on. As a result of concentrated attention to your outline, you should have become so familiar with it that if an incident you had planned begins to seem not quite right, you could try something else and revise the outline accordingly. Through this constant association with the outline, you will have already created well-imagined alternatives to your first tentative solutions.

If you accept your first story line and write the book accordingly, you are taking a great chance. Much happens in the course of writing any book or short story, much that is unexpected, and most of it good. For writing—and this is a crucial point—is a voyage of discovery. You cannot always tell where you are going, even though, like Columbus, you are quite certain of where you will end. Since this is a fact we have to accept, we must make allowances for those possible changes in direction.

The best place to make this allowance is in your outline, not after you have expended weeks, perhaps months, in writing chapters you now find you don't want. At that late stage, you will be most reluctant to make the radical changes needed. You may be too exhausted for such a task,

146

so you convince yourself to go along with what you have written. That is how bad books get sent to publishers.

In short, your outline is needed as much for finding out what won't work as it is for planning what will.

Do You Need an Outline for a Short Story?

With a short story, the problem is, of course, that you don't have as much room to work in as you do with the novel.

Compare writing the short story to painting a water color, and writing a novel to painting with oils. For the water colorist, each stroke counts for two, possibly three effects; and once the brush is put to paper, there is no going back over it. The touch must be light, deft, sure. Now take the oil painter. He makes a mistake. He wipes it off, then paints over and goes on. Working in oils, like writing the novel, is simply more forgiving of errors.

The short story has become a highly stylized, extremely individualized performance. Everything is compressed. A few words, like those brush strokes of the water colorist, must count for two, possibly three effects. The point must be made with great subtlety, the characterization accomplished with swift, clean strokes.

All of which means that you need to know precisely what you are about. Certainly you must know your theme, and a synopsis cannot but be of some help. After all, you proceed with the short story as you do with the novel, with the single exception that instead of breaking your synopsis into chapters, you divide it into scenes. And the outline will be much shorter, of course. Short or long, you need it for direction. If planning is vital for a novel, would it not be at least as important for writing that most deft construction, the short story? Yes, there are many successful writers who write short stories without the aid of outlines. But these are well-proven craftsmen. Are you quite sure you are that skilled already? If you think you are, then go ahead and write the short story without an outline. This is your choice to make.

Finally, the most important point of this chapter has been implied rather than stated: *Your outline is not something you write down as a chore and promptly forget. It is a living entity that grows as your novel grows, that stays with*

147

you, that serves as a constant goad and reminder of your story and of what you intend.

Think of it as a road map. Some drivers prefer to drive by the seat of their pants; others find it useful to know all the possible routes available for driving on to that other city.

Preparing Your Outline

1. Your opening is written by now; go over it, find your theme, and type up the outline of your novel or short story as described in this chapter. When you finish, hand it in to your instructor.

2. If, as sometimes happens, you no longer feel impelled to work on that opening you have already written, select or create a new main character and with him construct a new opening chapter or chapters and proceed as outlined: theme statement, short plot summary, division of summary into chapters or sections, and finally, the expansion of each chapter or section.

chapter fifteen

Believability

You are creating an illusion in the mind of the reader, but you wonder. Will he believe it? And it is a good question. If you're not good enough, of course, he won't. In this chapter you should get some useful hints concerning pace and detail that may go far toward making your story believable.

But Who'd Believe It?

Let's imagine that you have written a story for one of the men's mystery magazines, and the editor—a kindly fellow who took the time to comment on the rejection slip—wrote that he was unconvinced: "Too melodramatic, hard to believe."

Perhaps, in fact, you didn't really need him to tell you this. You had this same feeling yourself as you typed up the final draft. You knew you really had a lot of action, and the writing went well. But you, too, shook your head in a few places, wondering if anyone would really believe it.

Well, now you have your answer. The next question, obviously, is how can you make this figment of your imagination believable to the reader?

Too Much Happening?

The answer, surprisingly, may be that your story is just *too* exciting. A fast pace is important; but you can have too much happening—incidents and scenes coming in such rapid-fire order that it becomes rather ludicrous instead of exciting—like those speeded-up World War I news clips. The moment the reader senses this, he stops believing.

Suppose someone you knew had the following disasters overtake him in the space of two days: His car was stolen; his house burned to the ground, his little boy was seriously injured in a car accident, his job was lost to automation, and finally his wife decided to file for divorce.

"Oh, no!" you would have exclaimed as this last tidbit reached you. "I don't believe it!"

It makes no difference, of course, that such a sudden run of misfortune could bury any single one of us at any moment. You are writing fiction, remember, not copying the madcap world of reality. You must steer clear of that which *seems* unreal to the reader.

Redefine Incident

Well, you might ask, in some exasperation: How can you have excitement and crucial incidents if they are all going to be thought of as unbelievable melodrama by your reader? An answer comes through realizing that an incident, an exciting incident, can simply be a sudden change in the look a woman sends her lover. It can be the quality of a sigh—if that sigh has been awaited for more than a few pages. An exciting close to a scene or a chapter can be the description of the moon when the fellow watching it is contemplating going there. You can introduce menace simply by spending some time describing the piling up of thunderheads in the sky and the tense stillness hanging in the humid air.

Think of incident, then, in milder terms. Save your car crash and the fire. Perhaps you don't need them after all. The promise of disaster is sometimes more effective than the disaster itself.

Another answer to the problem of achieving believability is to slow down. Perhaps you are just skating over the top of your story, trying so hard to keep up the pace that you don't let the reader sink in to the events, to enjoy where he's been and what he's seen.

How to Slow Down

The solution may be to cut out some scenes entirely, and keep violent scenes offstage. Extend your dialogue a little, allowing your characters to be just a little more casual in their speech. Inject more local color, more detail concerning the background.

Here is where you need background information, for accurate detail is one of the most important devices you can use to make your story more believable. Read over what you have written and look for places where more specific facts concerning the lead character's town, where he works, and how he works could be fitted in.

151

If the lead character is a bank teller and the bulk of the action is in that bank, you will have to do considerable research on banks in order to get the feel of working in such a place. Then you will have to work to inject that "feel" into the narrative. It is this and sometimes only this that will make the bank teller's job believable to the reader.

Something else you might try if the pace is too swift, too melodramatic: Allow the reader to know what your character is thinking. What are his reactions to the events swirling about him? Tell the reader. Let him in on the lead character's ruminations. This might slow the pace just enough while still maintaining interest.

Believability Through Characterization

This leads us, finally, to perhaps your most important way of achieving believability: by characterizing more fully. Think a moment. When you see someone you do not know slip on a banana peel and dive into the gutter while his dog, leash trailing, goes yelping off through heavy traffic, you laugh. However, if you knew that person and understood that he had a weak heart, and that the dog was all he cared about since the death of his wife, what was funny a moment before, even slightly ludicrous, now would fill you with immediate concern.

What makes the difference?

The fact that you know the participant in the incident, of course. The more we know about people, it seems, the more we believe them and what happens to them. Take those poor people whose stories are recounted in the sensational weeklies. We can hardly believe what we read. And if we do, we just barely do, and without concern. In fact, we smile more often than not as we glance quickly over their stories. It is all so hopelessly melodramatic, like bad soap opera. If, however, we should happen to know one of the people we found ourselves reading about, we would then believe, and our laughter would become immediate concern.

Therefore, see your characters clearly, and see to it that by their actions they reveal themselves to your reader as well as they do to you. Primarily, it is character — not incident — that makes for believability in a short story or novel. If we do not believe in the people, we will not believe in what happens to them.

Theory into Practice

Now let's put all this advice together and see how it works in practice. First, we'll examine a scene from a mystery story in which the effect is so melodramatic as to make it — if not unbelievable — at least bordering on the unbelievable:

> As soon as Samson stepped out of the building, a knife whizzed past his face and buried itself in the doorway. He turned to look in the direction from which it came and saw a figure scuttling off into the darkness. Samson leaped after the man, caught him from behind, and flung him to the ground.

"Who are you, anyway?" Samson snarled. "Who sent you?"

But instead of answering, the man on the ground pulled a gun and fired. Samson felt the bullet strike him in the left shoulder. The bullet spun him around, momentarily dizzying him. He dropped to one knee, and when he looked up, his assailant was climbing into a car at the other end of the parking lot.

Shaking off nausea and dizziness, Samson raced back to his own car and climbed in and drove after the man. He did not catch up until the third light. Then he forced the other car toward the curb. There was an agonized scream from the brakes of his assailant's car as it jounced onto the sidewalk and crashed into a plate glass window.

Before the man could flee, Samson had him by the throat. "All right now. Tell me, punk. Who sent you?"

There is plenty of action in that sequence, all right, and a beginning writer might be pardoned for thinking that he really had something going for him. But of course all he's got going for him is bad melodrama that is not very convincing at all.

For one thing, it is too sketchy. There are very few details. What is the hero thinking all this time? And that bullet wound? Its effects are handled so skimpily that a participial phrase takes care of most of its description. The pace is so frantic, with so much happening in so short a time, that the reader gets at best only a vague impression of the action and the characters. In fact, the hero is characterized so slightly that he comes off as a faceless, emotionless Superman.

So let's slow the pace down some, add details in the narrative and in the background, and also to our characterization so as to make the hero less of a stick figure. Here is what we might get.

Samson stepped out of the building and paused. It was a nice quiet night. Too quiet, perhaps. He took out a new filter cigarette he was trying and lit it with the Ronson Jane had just bought him. A belated birthday gift, she had told him after the kiss. Snapping the lid shut, he dropped the lighter into his jacket pocket and felt its expensive heaviness. As the smoke filtered into his lungs, he remembered telling himself only that afternoon that he was going to have to quit smoking.

He'd live longer.

He caught the movement out of the corner of his eye; but even as he turned, the knife flashed out of the night, twinkling like a heavy butterfly past his nose, and buried itself in the wooden door jamb. The knife's blade was wedge-shaped, a professional throwing knife, he noted as, still turning, he saw a figure duck down behind a large black Cadillac.

He flicked the cigarette away, cut around the fin of the Cadillac, and with three quick strides overtook a figure scuttling ahead of him in the darkness. Grabbing at the struggling figure's right shoulder, he spun him violently. The knife thrower came around swinging. Samson ducked under a wild, roundhouse right, then bore in with a short left jab, following it up with a quick hard jab to the midsection, catching the fellow just under the breast bone. The man crumpled forward.

Samson caught him by the lapels of his maroon sports jacket and kept him upright. The man's thin face was sallow, greenish.

"Okay, fellow. Who sent you?"

The knife thrower collapsed suddenly forward into Samson's arms. The heady scent of jasmine momentarily clouded Samson's senses. The fellow was wearing a magenta shirt and tie, with a magenta handkerchief still tucked immaculately in his breast pocket. The handkerchief was the source of the jasmine.

Samson stepped back with a sigh and let the fellow fall to the macadam. Why in the hell, he thought, would Johnson send this creep after me? A knife thrower yet. Like something out of Fu Manchu, for Christ's sake.

Samson nudged him not so gently in the side with his foot. "Come on, fellow. Get up. I've got some questions."

Abruptly the fellow rolled over. Something exploded in his right hand, and Samson felt the white hot impact of the slug as it ripped into the fleshy part of his left shoulder. The force of the impact slammed him back against the Cadillac. A sudden nausea caused him to double over. He did not get sick, but he sagged to the pavement as it tipped crazily under him.

He heard the creep scrambling away and looked up in time to see him climb into a cream Corvette and roar off, his smoking tires squealing. Samson closed his eyes then, concentrated on keeping that last Scotch down, and got slowly to his feet. The upper shirtsleeve and the inside of his jacket were already heavy with his blood, and the shoulder ached like hell. He was hoping that—like in the movies—it would turn out to be only a flesh wound. He felt a little better as he made his way to his yellow Impala and climbed in painfully behind the wheel.

After Doc Winchell dug this slug out of his shoulder, he would have to take it easy for a while. But he would know what to look for when he was ready: a fragrant knife thrower who drove a cream Corvette. He wondered if Johnson was really that scared—to send one of his own boys after him like this.

If so, that meant he was getting closer to the truth than he had realized. He winced slightly as he turned to back his car out. . . .

Notice how the inclusion of details slows the pace. The lighter was given the hero as a belated birthday gift. The knife is wedge-shaped. The car the assailant ducks behind is a Cadillac.

The details carry over into the characterization. The knife thrower likes jasmine and magenta shirts. We know what Samson is thinking, a little something about the case he's working on, and even about his desire to quit smoking—a touch that should certainly make his appeal pretty close to universal. We can feel and share his incredulity at this audacious assault, thus taking much of the sting out of the melodramatic elements in the scene. The gunshot wound and its effects on Samson are treated in greater detail, while at the same time the number of incidents was cut by omitting that bit about the hero chasing his assailant's car and forcing him into a plate glass window.

The lead's characterization, then, is deepened and made more believable by relating not only what he does, but what he thinks, and even what he remembers. Details, all of them, but vitally important for achieving believability.

To sum up, you must keep your story moving, but not at the expense of believability. Too many incidents in too short a period of time, skimpy detail, both in terms of characterization and locale, give an air of unreality to the proceedings. The obvious remedy is to include more detail when describing the locale and when characterizing your people.

Too much violent action also lends an air of implausibility; thus, if possible, cut the number of violent incidents, especially those that take place in front of the reader. Incident is important, of course, but inhaling a cigarette and recalling a girl on a quiet night can be almost as intriguing as a knife thrown in the dark, especially when it allows the pace of the narrative to slow down enough to give the reader a chance to catch his breath.

In short, let the reader relax once in a while with the hero. With this in mind, create not only peaks of violent, conflict-provoking action, but occasional valleys of quieter moments as well. Surely you remember what it was like when the roller coaster, between headlong plunges, gathered itself and crept slowly up the next grade, giving you the chance to look far out over the beach and the great blue platter of ocean beyond. That momentary lull was easily as delicious as the wild fall down the other side.

Putting This Chapter to Work for You

You have already written the opening chapter of your novel or the opening sequence in your short story. You remembered that you should not lose your reader and included much action. Now check to see if the action is too fast, so fast-moving, in fact, as to be ludicrous. One of the best ways to determine this is to read what you have written aloud to someone—your fellow writers, certainly; but anyone will do for this, for it is what *you* hear that matters more than anything else at this point. And if it is ludicrous, you'll hear it— as well as see it on the faces of your listeners.

If the pace is too fast, go back to your desk and follow some of the hints suggested in this chapter. Cut some of the incidents. Describe some things a bit more fully than you had. Avoid fuzzy generalizations when specifics will make the object and the locale more real.

Check your characterization. Have you described your main character's physical appearance? Is he presented sympathetically—as a human being, with his share of faults as well as with traits you might admire?

Next you should check your dialogue. Surprisingly, most beginners try to speed their story along and enhance interest by including lots and lots of dialogue. As a result, much of the dialogue is hopelessly boring and, for the most part, entirely unnecessary. When it does not characterize as well as provide information the reader must have, dialogue should be struck.

After you have gone over your opening with these criticisms in mind, rewrite where you have to, saving the first version. Then either present these two versions to your instructor or read them aloud to your classmates to see if you have indeed improved your first version and have escaped having what you write dismissed as unbelievable.

If your instructor or your fellow students give you the go-ahead, go back to the desk and finish your story or the opening chapters of your novel. If you are working on a novel and have not yet written your outline, stop after four chapters and get to work on it. Don't go beyond four chapters without an outline. If you do, you run the risk of getting hopelessly muddled—and dangerously discouraged.

chapter sixteen

Rewriting

"*I have never thought of myself as a good writer. Anyone who wants reassurance of that should read one of my first drafts. But I'm one of the world's great rewriters.*

"*I find that three or four readings are required to comb out the clichés, line up pronouns with their antecedents, and insure agreement in number between subject and verbs. . . . My connectives, my clauses, my subsidiary phrases don't come naturally to me and I'm very prone to repetition of words; so I never even write an important letter in the first draft. I can never recall anything of mine that's ever been printed in less than three drafts.*

"*You write that first draft really to see how it's going to come out.*"

JAMES A. MICHENER

By now you have had ample time to get to know your characters, to work over your plot outline so as to catch any holes in it, and finally to come to grips with the actual writing of your story or novel. Now you come to the moment of truth: rewriting. In this chapter you will be shown not only why you should rewrite but, I hope, how to rewrite. What follows, admittedly, may not be the final, definitive method for rewriting as far as you are concerned, but for now it is the only method you have. It has worked for other writers as well as for me. Use it until you devise a better way.

Once you've got that first draft written, taken that amorphous, insubstantial phantom of a story, and put it down on paper—real at last, tangible finally—you can begin the next great struggle: revision.

Writing is Rewriting

I used the term "struggle" and I meant it, for revision is wrestling with a demon—and that demon is yourself. But there is no escape, for anyone can write—and almost everyone you meet these days is writing. However, only the writers know how to rewrite. It is this ability alone that turns the amateur into a professional.

Rewriting can be very exciting. It is most satisfying to see your story grow under your red pencil, to see the excesses pruned, the lovely sentences struck out, the sweet but useless adjectives swept ruthlessly away, some characters altered, others annihilated without a qualm—in short, to bring order out of the chaos that is the first draft.

Get Rid of You

Some beginning writers, however, do not see it this way. They shrink back in horror at the very mention of rewriting. To them, that first draft is something utterly remarkable, immutable even, a creation that must not be changed in any way. This, however, is a dangerous delusion they must get over—fast. That first draft is invariably bad, filled with posturing, with overblown descriptions—in a word, you.

Yes, you. Rewriting is, more often than not, simply the art of excising oneself, which means that you must get rid of your favorite phrases and your stunning descriptions, especially those that reveal your truly poetic nature. Cross out that profound observation you've wanted to see in print for years now and that ironic comment you slipped in, the one that made you chuckle so at your cleverness. Cross it out! Cross them all out—all the vestiges of your ego.

I am not exaggerating. In fact, what I have found quite often is that those passages on which I had lavished the most time as I wrote—hunting up synonyms, revising sentences, striking out words—were passages that were dead to begin with and needed to be taken out entirely. Invariably they were instances of my own intrusion. Either I was in love with the passage: I had always wanted to write a description of a sunset at sea, for instance; or the passage didn't really belong there in the first place and was just something I wanted to put in to satisfy my writer's vanity. So out it went.

Revise for Clarity

If the first thing you must do when you revise is to cut yourself out of the text, the next is to clarify. This clarity is what you owe your reader above all else.

You may be ambiguous about your story's ultimate meaning, the significance of it all. This is to be expected. But what is happening on stage—who the characters are, what their names are, what they say when they speak, what they are wearing, what time of day it is—all of this must be made perfectly clear to the reader. Where is the phone? On a night stand, on the wall, or sitting on the floor near the bed? Is it a check or a plaid she is wearing, a cape or an overcoat? Is the collar imitation fur or real mink? Make it clear.

Clarify with short, deft strokes. Don't clutter. To clarify does not mean to choke the story with insignificant detail. Add; then prune. Clarify; then prune. Keep it simple, direct. Art is in knowing what to leave out as well as what to put in.

In order to accomplish this, you must know what point you are trying to make with each scene, character, and plot development, which means in turn that your theme must be kept in mind all during this revision. Otherwise you will have no yardstick by which to measure what stays in, what comes out, or what you must add. Every bit of description, every article the character owns, his actions, the words he utters—all are a reflection of the point your story is making, *or should be making.*

Meanwhile, keep going. Don't get bogged down on one page. If you do, you will get so sick and tired of your story that you will lose all perspective, all attachment and sympathy for your characters and their story. Somehow, then, you must learn to know when it is best to leave the page you are working on and go on to the next scene, to let well enough alone. Later you'll be able to return to it and see it more clearly.

A Check List of Some Things to Look For

Clean out the adjective pairs, the repetitions. You'll find them all over. Look for favorite words, phrases, mannerisms, purple patches, overwriting, any passages where you were fuzzy when you should have been clear.

An example of this last would be: "The room was cluttered with all sorts of things." *What* sorts of things were in the room and where were they? On shelves, bookcases, window casements? Name some of the items specifically, picking out a few to indicate the general type. This kind of hazy generalization is meaningless cotton candy that reduces to nothing once the reader tries to take it in.

It may not make the events or the characters in your story any clearer by getting rid of this kind of phrasing, but it will get rid of lazy, inept writing. If you're going to describe the items in the room, the car, or the dress, then *do* it. Otherwise, forget it. Leave the description out entirely.

Go over the grammar, the punctuation, the sentences that aren't sentences. Watch out for the comma fault or splice. If you don't know what these terms mean, get a handbook of grammar and make it your business to find out.

Go over the spelling. Any word you wouldn't be willing to bet your life on as being correctly spelled is probably incorrect. So look it up.

Style

A short word here about style. Essentially it boils down to this: Don't worry about it. If you have planned your writing intelligently, if you have built your characters as solidly as you should have, if your story has begun to take hold, then relax. Undoubtedly the quality of your style has been something that did not occur to you as you busied yourself telling your story. You were too busy to worry about metaphors, similes, use of adjectives and adverbs, parallelisms, and so on.

What you *were* worrying about was whether or not you were telling your story as clearly and as simply as you could. If you did accomplish this—and you will know after you finish your revision—you will find that your style has taken care of itself. It got the job done. That is all a style is supposed to do.

Remember that you are an individual. No matter what you may do to change those unique characteristics that make you indubitably yourself and no one else, you can't. The same is true of your style. Your writing style is your own, an expression of whatever individuality you possess. This is true no matter how long or how hard you might labor to write like someone else.

Just keep in mind that as long as you relate clearly and simply what you see in your mind's eye, you will be exhibiting your style. If the reader is moved and the story has a nice pace and your characters come alive, your style is in fine working order.

Reading the Manuscript Through

Once you have gone through the story or the four opening chapters of your novel correcting for clarity and mechanical faults such as spelling and sentence structure, paragraphing, and so on, go back and read straight through the manuscript without touching a word.

Try to get the feel of it, the pulse; see how it flows, where it lags—try to become not yourself, but a stranger who has just picked this story up and is glancing through it trying to decide whether or not to read it.

As you read, ask yourself if the opening grabs you, pulls you into the story. Then ask yourself if you are interested in or bored by your characters, especially the lead character. Do you really care what happens to them? Be brutally honest with yourself on this point, for these questions concerning your characters are the most important you can ask. You are creating people; and unless they are interesting, what happens to them will not be of any concern to the reader.

This is what you read for then. The characters. They must intrigue you. And they must be consistent.

After the Read-through

Now that you've read through the story or the opening chapters, you should have gathered certain general impressions.

There are obviously characters that need work, places where the story bogs down or races ahead too fast. Where it lags, you will cut—ruthlessly. Where it races ahead, you will zoom in closer and give detail to make things more vivid, more real. And where your characters seem too dim or act inconsistently, you will really have to go to work.

Sometimes it will help to change the name of a character that does not seem right. Other times you may be justified in getting rid of him entirely. You may have left out pertinent information about this person, information that *you* know and that helps to make him live for you, but that you failed to pass on to your reader. One hint here: A man is what he dreams, what he fears, what he loves—as well as what he wears, how he walks and how he talks.

Fitting in the Corrections

The question of how to manage all these corrections is a good one. Where do you put all this rewriting, and how do you fit it into the manuscript? It's a real problem in logistics, handling all this extra text without getting hopelessly confused as you turn that nice neat manuscript into a tangled nightmare of crossed-out words, arrows, and indecipherable corrections.

First of all, try to do all of your corrections on the pages you have typed. Write in whatever additions you have in the margins with arrows from the text indicating where they go. At first glance it will look impossible to follow, but your story line will prevent you from getting lost. Then if you need still more room for corrections, use the other side of the paper. Occasionally you will add a new scene or a completely rewritten scene in longhand to the pages.

A good move at this juncture would be to invest in a looseleaf notebook, if you haven't already done so for the outline. Use that three-hole punch I mentioned earlier, take your manuscript, punch holes in the pages, and enclose the manuscript in the notebook along with the outline. Then you can take those pages you have rewritten and click them into the notebook with the rest of the manuscript.

Then keep correcting and keep going.

You do all this quietly, curled up in a corner somewhere, lost in your characters and their story. When you have finished, you will have a notebook filled with those pages from which you will type the final draft, pages that only you, most probably, will be able to read.

The Third Revision

Now you are ready to start typing up the final copy, either of your short story or of those four opening chapters and outline. I suggest, at this point, that you use erasable bond. It will go slowly. As you type, you will find yourself stopping at a word to consider if this is really the one you want. You will begin making corrections of your corrections.

Sometimes you will push the typewriter away, grab a sheet of blank paper, and proceed to rewrite a scene from scratch. You will polish it carefully, take a deep breath, and then type it up as part of your final draft. And so it will go as this final draft becomes, in effect, your third draft. And it will all be done with incredible care and attention to detail because you will know that this is the copy that goes out to the editor.

When you have finished, you should find that some passages are fresh off the top of your head, while others have been gone over time and again as you ripped page after page out of the typewriter and tried again. Yet, when you read it over for typing errors, you will find that it all hangs together perfectly.

165

Sounds risky. Okay, so it is, but this is how to do it if you don't want to lose yourself in endless revisions.

What About Hiring a Typist?

Recently a would-be writer explained to me that as soon as he found a typist to type up the rough draft of his novel, he would send me the book so my agent could make him rich. I told him I would not look at anything he wrote unless he typed up the final draft himself. It is my considered opinion that hiring a typist is the worst possible way to handle the final draft.

If you will note, I am assuming that this draft is also a

revision, one that takes place in a white heat of concentration. No typist—no matter how skilled or sympathetic—can do this for you. Some of your most crucial revisions, many that may make the difference between success and failure, occur during the typing of that final send-to-the-editor copy. Remember, the key here is that you know that this is it, the last copy; there will be no more chances to revise, no typist to complete this onerous task. It's all up to you, and the time is now. It is this knowledge that accounts for the concentration that makes it work. You are putting yourself through a wringer, it is true, but there is really no other way.

Therefore, send your manuscript to a typist at your own peril; I cannot understand how any writer who really takes pride in his work could allow himself to step aside at this juncture.

You need to rewrite, then, to get rid of your own posturing, to clear up the grammar, the spelling, to strike out all the nonessentials, the clutter—and above all to clarify. In the end, all you should have are your characters and their story, as clearly and as simply presented as you can manage it.

Anyone can write; only the writers can rewrite. Here is where the job gets done, where the crucial struggle is fought. And no one can do it for you—not the typist or the editor of the magazine.

This is *your* story. It's up to you to make it good.

Now That You've Finished the First Draft

Read aloud to one of your classmates, or to your instructor, your short story or the first four chapters of your novel. And listen—along with your fellow sufferers—for the following:

1. Too many adjectives, repetitious words, overworked phrases, personal mannerisms, overwriting in general.
2. Unnecessarily involved sentences, poor sentence structure, rambling sentences, paragraphs that go on too long.
3. The dramatic potential of the scenes not fully realized.
4. Lack of clarity, too many generalities.
5. Confusing transitions.
6. Dialogue not clearly tagged.
7. Lack of important information needed for understanding.

A discussion should then be initiated along the following general lines: Are the characters clearly drawn? Do we feel with them? Is what happens to them important to us? Are we moved by their fate—to laughter, tears, a sense of irony?

What does the story or novel tell us about people—about life in general? Does it all amplify the theme? How appropriate is the title?

After this discussion you should go back to your desk and make the necessary revisions in your manuscript and then type up the final draft. This will take some time, and it would be a fine idea if your instructor did not let you back into class until you had typed your final send-to-the-editor draft.

It should be understood by now—and reiterated, I am sure, by your instructor—that if you have chosen to write a novel, your final draft will contain only the four chapters and the outline, while if you chose to write a short story, you should be working on the final draft of the completed story.

Both the novel and short story will be sent out if you complete them to the satisfaction of your instructor—the short story to an appropriate magazine, the four chapters and outline to a publisher. In submitting novels today, this is the accepted procedure, since publishers prefer queries first and then want to see only the opening chapters and the outline.

Do not feel, incidentally, that because you are only submitting four chapters and an outline that you will not have to revise and fuss over this submission as much as you would for a completed novel. Most of my novels, including *167* my last one, were sold this way. And this last manuscript, consisting of four chapters and an extensive outline—containing in all 127 pages—was revised completely at least twice.

But more about submitting your manuscript in the next chapter.

chapter seventeen

You have now finished your final draft. Where do you send it; and how do you address the manuscript? What about rights? This chapter is designed to help answer these questions.

As discussed earlier in this text, book publishers and magazines are going more and more to nonfiction; less and less do they expect their fiction to carry them any distance at all. It is to their nonfiction lists that book publishers look for solvency, and in most magazines today the articles, not the fiction, are what get the full treatment on the cover.

Query First

Because of the situation regarding fiction today, the rules regarding submission of book manuscripts as well as short stories are undergoing a subtle change. No longer, in many of the magazines and publishing houses, for instance, will editors read unsolicited novels or short stories.

They prefer a query letter first, asking if they would care to see your book or story. If they like the tone of your letter, they will ask you to send along the story or a few sample chapters and an outline if the work is a novel.

Out of fifteen paperback book publishers of original fiction, eleven now prefer queries, followed by sample chapters and outline. The percentage is not so high as yet with hardcover publishers, but it seems to be rising rapidly.

Of those hardcover publishers who do, however, many are major houses: Bernard Geis, Harcourt Brace Jovanovich, Dodd Mead, Scribners, Macmillan. And the tone is getting fairly shrill. A Scribners' editor says, "Authors should not submit manuscripts without prior correspondence." The editor of Hill and Wang wrote, "Authors *must* query before submitting."

This is a significant trend because it is so unusual. At one time magazine and book publishers counted on the fact that all they had to do was open their doors and the manuscripts—unsolicited—would come pouring in "over the transom," as they called it. They automatically supplied the junior editors needed to read them as part of the daily routine of publishing.

What has happened now, some say, is that books of a purely general—that is, nondirected—interest do not sell well, with fiction selling the poorest of all. Thus the solution, as they see it, is to save money by cutting down on their first and second line readers, then to go out and find the people to write the book, article, or short story they feel already has a market because of the sudden interest in a given topic: occultism, astrology, ecology, and so on.

In the course of a discussion I had with the editor of a major publisher, I was moved to remark that his attitude toward fiction seemed somewhat negative, that one almost felt apologetic when discussing fictional projects with him. He agreed. He had a few novels in the hopper that would soon have to be published, books on which he had already advanced considerable sums, but he was not happy at the prospect.

Evidently publishing fiction these days—except for the occasional blockbuster or Book-of-the-Month-Club selection or movie tie-in—is tantamount to dropping a pebble into the Pacific. The book just disappears. The track record for first novels, of course, is especially depressing.

This, then, is the reason for the query letter. It prevents the magazines and the book editors from being inundated with a tide of manuscripts that they no longer have the staff or the inclination to wade through. They now see only the work of those authors they choose to see. Though Viking recently published a first novel found in the slush pile, the important thing to remember about this was the furor such an event aroused in the publishing world—as well as the numbing fact that this was the first time in 26 years that a publishable novel had reached Viking by this route.

The query letter an established author would send out differs, of course, from that which an unknown writer with no previous publications would submit. For instance, here's a query letter I sent out to a number of editors when I decided to try my hand at writing westerns:

25 South Main Street
Winterhaven, New York
October 25, 1973

Joanmarie Tremont
Editor
Tellmor Productions, Inc.
185 Madison Avenue
New York, N. Y.

Dear Ms. Tremont:

Under my pseudonym, Bill J. Carol, I have published over thirty books in the past eleven years, mostly teen-age sports and mysteries, with one science-fiction book to give the mix some spice.

I am listed — as who isn't — in Contemporary Authors and Something About the Author, am a member of SFWA and the Author's Guild.

Since I am moving now into the adult category paperback field, I would like to send you the opening four chapters and an outline of my western TASTE OF VENGEANCE. If there are categories within categories, I would have to say this western is of the classic variety.

Would you be interested in seeing the chapters and the outline?

Sincerely,

I have changed the name of the editor and the publishing house, but nothing else in the above letter. At the time, I sent out individually typed copies of this letter to every paperback publisher that published westerns, addressing each letter to the appropriate editor in charge of that category, information I was able to obtain with little difficulty in *Writer's Market*.

I was fortunate in getting a single response from an editor. I sent her the chapters and outline and she bought the book — and has since bought others.

Notice that it was a neat, business letter and that though I sent out many copies of this letter, each one was individually typed and addressed to the editor involved. Even if the editor to whom you address your query is no longer with the publisher — and this happens quite often — the letter will be forwarded to the editor now filling that post, an editor new on the job and quite likely on the alert for new writers.

Or at least so you must hope.

But how, you ask, should the unpublished writer go about writing a query letter? Well, for one thing, your letter will be somewhat shorter:

25 Burbank Street
Boston, Massachusetts
October 31, 1977

Harry Sheldon
Editor
Tellmor Productions, Inc.

185 Madison Avenue
New York, N. Y.

Dear Mr. Sheldon:

I am currently working on a novel dealing with the emergence
of the American Indian in today's society. Close on the heels of
the Black Revolution, it seems, is the Red Revolution. The
protagonist of my book—an American Indian of the Seneca
tribe in New York State—finds himself trying to articulate his
new found awareness of his ancestry, his heritage in the face of
parental indifference and hostility. The effect of all this on his
marriage and on his ties to his children and the surrounding
community of Fall River makes up the bulk of the book.

Would you be interested in seeing the opening four chapters
and an outline?

Sincerely,

Again, the letter is a neat business letter with heading
and so on. It is not a handwritten note. It is short and con-
cise, telling the editor what he would need to know in order
to judge whether or not the subject matter and treatment
would fit into his current publishing plans. If, for instance,
he just finished editing for publication a book dealing with
the Indian problem, he would not be likely to want to see
another novel dealing with the same material so soon after.

The businesslike tone of the letter, its neatness and the
fact that not a single word was misspelled are all in its favor,
that and the succinct summary of what you propose to submit. Nothing else is required, nor needed. Since you have
not published anything, you cannot cite your publications,
so you say nothing on this score—and you certainly do *not*
volunteer any information that would turn the editor off,
such as the fact that you are a student anxious to have such
a prestigious publishing firm publish your first novel, or that
your mother read the book from start to finish and couldn't
put it down, and so on.

If you have published nothing, your query letter should
be as straightforward and brief as the sample above. Anything longer or more detailed—in short a query that would
take up too much of the editor's time—would only act
against you.

Let's assume you receive a go-ahead from the editor. If
you do, here's what it will most likely look like:

Dear Mr. Wilson:

Thank you very much for your letter of October 31st.

We would very much like to see the four opening chapters and outline of your novel INDIAN LORE. Mr. Sheldon is no longer with us, so would you kindly mark the package to my attention.

Sincerely,

Amanda Blakiston
Associate Editor

And that's it. Send the book out. You've got an editor on the other end of that line already interested. So don't waste any time at all.

Behind Editorial Doors

Will your stories or books be read? Of course they will. The publishing houses and magazines need your work in order to have something to sell to the market. You supply their life-blood; you are the reason for their continued existence. So don't fret. The editors will read what you send them.

What happens when your manuscript arrives at the publishers? Depending on the size of the publishing house or magazine, it may be anyone from the junior first reader on up to the vice president who will open your manuscript and begin to read. Usually it is the first reader, some young man or woman fresh out of college with a degree in English literature, hoping that it is your manuscript that will help him or her make it big in the editorial world.

Let's assume that this first reader does not gag on your opening paragraph, that the reader likes your story very much. Okay. It is then sent along to another, more senior reader—and the book or story starts up the editorial ladder. If it remains alive, it finally arrives on the desk of the senior editor; and from there—if he or she likes it—it is considered at a monthly or weekly conference in which all of those in charge of production, sales, and editorial policy take part. If the book or story passes muster at this conference, you are sent a letter containing a check if it's a story, or a contract and a small advance — anywhere from five hundred to a couple of thousand — if it's a book.

How long does all this take? As you can imagine, this whole process requires quite a bit of time. Obviously, on small magazines or publishing houses that editorial chain of command is much shorter, and it seems reasonable therefore to expect a much prompter decision. But don't bet on it. A decision on a short story can take anywhere from four to six weeks, for a novel seven weeks to seven months, or longer.

Usually you can assume that if the editors take longer than this, they are considering your manuscript quite seriously. On the other hand, they might have lost it or the publishing house might be in the throes of an editorial changeover. Whatever the cause, it is always a long, long wait for the writer, and one that only seldom ends happily. One consolation: If your manuscript is really bad, it might come back within a week or two.

Once the editors have made their decision, it is final. There is no appeal. All you can do when your manuscript comes back is send it out to another publisher or to another magazine — and keep on resubmitting it until there are no more publishers or magazines to whom you can send your manuscript. Only then should you finally decide to put the book or story away as unpublishable.

Multiple Submissions

At one time xeroxing your manuscript and sending it out to more than one publisher was not a good idea. Although some authors had been doing this for years, they were the Big Names, the proven writers the publishers knew would sell, the fellows who had publishers sandbagging each other to get them onto their lists.

If you, an unknown, sent in a Xeroxed copy of your manuscript, the editor would promptly send it back without reading it. Why should he go through all the trouble of reading your work, taking it up the editorial ladder to the senior editor, defending it in conference, sending out a contract and letter of acceptance, only to find that someone else had already purchased the manuscript? It was a good point — at the time.

Fortunately, this policy has undergone what can only be described as a seismic change. More and more, editors — when they list their requirements — are admitting that they *will* consider photo copied manuscript, even though these manuscripts may represent multiple submissions. I suggest you check first to make sure which houses will consider multiple submissions and take advantage of this breakthrough when submitting your book.

Should Your Story or Book Be Copyrighted Before You Submit It?

Don't worry about publishers stealing what you send them. They get your life's blood cheap enough without having to steal it. Of all the bogeymen that frighten young writers, this is the most common and the most silly.

As far as short stories go, don't worry about North American Serial Rights, South American, or anything in between. The editor will tell you what rights he is purchasing when he sends you the acceptance letter. When your book is published, it will automatically be copyrighted in your name or that of your publisher—it makes little difference which at this stage.

Where to Send Your Manuscript

Purchase copies of *The Writer* or *Writer's Digest*, two journals for writers that contain market lists of magazine and book publishers, with short comments by the editors as to their needs of the moment. If you do not wish to purchase these magazines, the local library should have copies you can study. But you *must* do this. You must study the market lists yourself.

176

If you have written a short story, you search these lists carefully and select a magazine that seems to be in the market for the kind of story you have written. Then you send the completed manuscript—enclosing a self-addressed, stamped envelope—to the magazine you have chosen and get busy on your next short story. In marketing your short story, do not overlook the small, college literary magazines. Though they do not pay, they publish many stories in the course of the year, and editors of major publishers are constantly reading their issues on the lookout for promising young writers. If you can establish a reputation in these magazines, you might well be on your way.

But remember, almost the only way you are going to learn about these magazines is to study the listings, not only in the two writer's journals mentioned above, but also in the

Writer's Market published by *Writer's Digest* in Cincinnati, and *The Writer's Handbook,* published by *The Writer* in Boston. Indeed, it has always astonished me to find how many people sincerely interested in writing there are who do not know of the existence of these magazines and publications. It surprises me because I know of no other way — short of journeying to the offices of these magazines or calling up the editors personally — for the writer who does not have an agent to find the names, addresses and requirements of the magazines which might be interested in publishing his or her work.

If it is a novel you have written, you find a publisher who appears to be in the market for your kind of book — experimental, serious adult, gothic, western, detective — and write a query letter to the appropriate editor. If you get an okay, you send in the chapters and outline, being sure to include return postage. Also, it is advisable that you make certain your name and address appear on the cover page and the last page. And, of course, you will make sure that it is a tight, neat packaging job.

You can send the book special fourth class rate special handling; and the rates are very reasonable. However, you might prefer to send all your manuscripts first class. This will ensure their getting to the publisher sometime during the latter half of this century. Indeed, more and more writers are sending their manuscripts by United Parcel Service. The UPS seems to be as quick and not much more expensive than the postal service.

If you enclose a covering letter with the manuscript, simply remind the editor that this is the novel he or she has requested to see as a result of your letter. Anything else would be superfluous. Remember, always, the less you say, the better.

Your manuscript must speak for you.

What Do You Do While Waiting?

Some beginning writers make the mistake of banking on that first book or short story so greatly that when they finish it and send it out, they camp by the mailbox for the next three to six months, waiting not so patiently for the mailman to bring them that long envelope containing the contract and a hefty check.

This is a mistake, a very bad mistake. You will break

the pattern of your writing during this long wait. You will get increasingly anxious. Paranoid. Are they stealing your story? Friends will begin to notice your odd ways. Previously you were satisfyingly invisible. Everyone admired your perseverance. Now you stumble about in everybody's way as you search the horizon for the mailman, and natter constantly about that damned book or short story you wrote.

You have become a pest, a nuisance to yourself and to those about you.

Get back to that desk and begin on your next project. If you sent out the opening chapters of a novel, get busy on the rest of it. Since you should have either a carbon copy or a xerox copy of everything you send out, you can work from your copy of the novel and go on from where you left off. If it was a short story, set to work on your next one. Once you do this, you will be startled and gratified to find how rapidly you will forget all about that manuscript going the rounds.

By the time that short story comes back, you'll be so wrapped up in your second story — or third — that you'll only shrug, think the editors were crazy for not taking it, and promptly send it out again. Then you will return to your desk just a little annoyed at the interruption. And the same if it's a novel. You'll send out more query letters and then get on with finishing the book.

That's a writer.

Now That You Are Ready to Market Your Manuscript

1. If your manuscript is a novel, select a publisher. Once you have done this, type up your query letter and send it out. If you get an affirmative response, pack your four chapters and outline securely, enclosing enough postage for the return trip, and checking to make sure your name and address are typed on the first and last pages of the manuscript. If this is to be a multiple submission, then make as many Xerox copies as you will need and repeat this process with each publisher you select.

2. If your manuscript is a short story, select a magazine and send the completed story to the appropriate editor of that publication, enclosing a stamped self-addressed envelope. Use the large manila envelopes for your manuscript. Mail the story flat. Folding it and stuffing it into an envelope, no matter how short the story might be, is never a good

idea. You may, of course, fold the return manila envelope once in order to fit it into the envelope containing the manuscript.

3. Discuss with the other members of your class where you have sent your manuscript—and what you are going to work on next. If you have just sent in four chapters and an outline, you've got your work cut out for you. In about three months an editor might ask for the rest of your book. You'd better be ready if he does.

Or, perhaps you are busy already on another short story.

chapter eighteen

Now That You Are a Writer

"*Perhaps it would be better not to be a writer, but if you must, then write. If all feels hopeless, if that famous "inspiration" will not come, write. If you are a genius, you'll make your own rules, but if not — and the odds are against it — go to your desk no matter what your mood, face the icy challenge of the paper — write.*"

J. B. PRIESTLY

By this time you should be hooked. If so, this final chapter should confirm your awareness of your commitment — and its challenge.

I hope that by the time you have reached this chapter, you will have been hard at work on another short story or finishing up that novel. If fortune is kind and you work diligently, you'll complete it within a reasonable time, less than a year perhaps.

Naturally, you don't know if it will sell. It might very well be sent back with humiliating haste. Yet you continue to write, buoyed by hope one moment, plunged into self-doubt the next—always naggingly aware that this whole business just might be a monstrous waste of time—a towering boondoggle.

Some Random Comments

Yes, it is a lonely frustrating way to make your fortune, and I sometimes wonder why so many people are attempting it.

But despite the loneliness and the frustration, however, there are still the twin compensations: the exhilaration of conception and the joy of accomplishment.

It is the long, arid stretches between these two points where the trouble lies; for invariably during that long trek your most constant companion is bleak discouragement. Many writers will confirm this fact and point out that there was almost always a point at which they simply did not know how they could possibly go on. And yet they finished the book or story, and the memory of that despair faded.

What makes it all worthwhile must be the challenge. Consider what you are attempting to do—create a world of your own, populated by the children of your imagination. Such a task must dominate your life, possess you completely.

Writer friends of mine have often agreed with me whenever I wondered what in the world others did with their time if they didn't write. The answer—perhaps—is that they are looking for that same sense of purpose the writer enjoys.

If you've gotten this far, you might very well have that sense of purpose. Unfortunately, it might not be enough. I have known people who have written constantly all their lives without success. Two of them filled countless loose-leaf notebooks with pages upon pages of narrative. They wore out typewriters. They kept at it doggedly year after year, the sound of their clacking typewriters the only music, the only solace they seemed to need. Each of them died without a word of theirs seeing the light of a published page. It must have been like carrying on an urgent, lifelong conversation with someone they loved desperately, who yet remained — throughout it all — completely indifferent.

Then there are those who publish the first book they write, as did a student of mine in an adult education class a few years back.

Does It Get Any Easier

By this time, I hope, the monkey is on your back. You have established a writing schedule. You now expect to write at a certain hour each day; and you become restless when that time rolls around and you are not at your desk. You are getting steadily more proficient in terms of grammar and punctuation — and more aware of people and their stories. Your life is filled, and soon the book or short story you are working on now will be finished.

But then there will be the next one, and the next one, with each story or book as difficult or more difficult than the one before. You'll be surprised at this perhaps, then resigned.

It never gets easier.

How can this be? Surely you will have learned much during those early abortive efforts at story-telling. Those struggles with plotting, characterization, grammar, and spelling should finally become a thing of the past. To a certain extent, this is true. But what happens is that you become steadily more demanding of yourself. You will want to tighten your descriptive passages, improve your pacing, and you will give yourself in each new book or story a technical problem that has to be solved — one that will really challenge you. You will try tricky points of view, or perhaps you will experiment with fast cuts, unusual transitions, or a theme difficult to dramatize in terms of story.

In short, you can't be satisfied as easily as you once were. You'll read over old manuscripts and wonder how you could have considered sending them out for publication. And if you do manage to sell a few books or stories, you'll be appalled at how poorly they read. You have gone beyond that point, you see.

What Do You Do When It Becomes a Grind?

Some writers who have the time and the money periodically escape to places of refuge to rest their pens. Others take up outdoor hobbies: golfing, fishing, hunting, boating. They do this frantically, I notice, in an effort to escape the grind — a vain effort.

Sure, it helps some. The trouble is that a writer can never escape his task; for no matter where he goes, he carries within him the source of his unrest — his creative imagination. Like an immortal swarm of bees trapped within his skull, it never rests.

The best thing is to try to make the most of it. Write in comfortable surroundings. Take that loose-leaf notebook with you to a bar or an all-night cafeteria. Write with your feet resting in a swift-running brook. Get away from the desk. I write in my den while listening to music through earphones so as not to disturb my family.

It doesn't *seem* like such a grind then.

The Writer's Life

As you must have realized by now, the life of the writer is not exactly as it is portrayed in the motion pictures; though for the Big Names, of course, it can be a pretty luxurious existence.

Yet all a writer really needs is some fresh bond, a scratch notebook, a typewriter, some solitude, and a mail box to be in business.

There *is* a certain freedom about a writer's life that is most appealing, especially to those viewing it from the outside; and for the writer who can earn enough to live in reasonable comfort, the life can be pretty close to ideal. For those who cannot make enough to support themselves by their writing alone, this ideal is a constant goal toward which they struggle.

Yet the average writer's life is much as it has been pictured in this text. Hard, unremitting effort for long years in the privacy of a den, while the rest of the world joins clubs, goes to movies, devours TV, or takes long summer trips out West.

Fame

On this subject I can speak with very little authority. Oh, sure, the grocer and my colleagues know I write books, and school librarians, bless them, are always glad to have me visit and talk to the youngsters they've shanghaied into joining their library club.

But that's it. And it's enough. For the writer, fame should never be considered an end in itself. At best it is a dangerous distraction that does not have to destroy, but that will very often cause some damage. For one thing, fame robs you of the anonymity you should prize as a writer. Once you are set apart as a creature different from the common run—a distressing attitude most people fall into when regarding a writer—it is difficult if not impossible for you to regain that easy relationship you once enjoyed with your neighbors and friends. Yet you must have this easy access to them if you are to continue to write about people in your fiction. Thus fame can cut you off from the very source of your work.

Of course, the great writers of the past were able to handle the special problems created by fame. But the point is that fame *does* cause problems, and if there is one thing a writer does not need, it is another obstacle to overcome.

So forget completely about fame. Monetary success is fine. With this you can continue to write. But fame should not be your primary goal. All you should be concerned with as you write is how well you are liberating those children of your imagination.

Goodbye Now

I hope that somewhere within these pages you found what you needed to help you proceed a few steps further along the path you have chosen. If so, I am gratified.

Good luck.

bibliography

For the Writer's Desk

Adkins, Rose and Jane Koester. *Writer's Market.* Cincinnati: *Writer's Digest,* 1977.

Bernstein, Theodore M. *The Careful Writer: A Modern Guide to English Usage.* New York: Atheneum, 1965.

Burack, A. S., ed. *The Writer's Handbook.* Boston: The Writer, 1977.

Fowler, H. W. *Modern English Usage.* Rev. Sir Ernest Gowers. New York: Oxford University Press, 1965.

Follett, Wilson. *Modern American Usage,* ed. Jacques Barzun. New York: Hill & Wang, 1966.

Strunk, William J., and E.B. White. *The Elements of Style.* New York: Macmillan, 1959.

What the Writers Have To Say

Allen, Walter E., ed. *Writers on Writing.* Boston: The Writer, 1959.

Allott, Miriam, ed. *Novelists on the Novel.* New York: Columbia University Press, 1959.

Bowen, Elizabeth. *Seven Winters and Afterthoughts.* New York: Alfred Knopf, 1962.

Cowley, Malcolm & George Plimpton, ed. *Writers at Work* ("The Paris Review Interviews"). Series 1–4. New York: Viking, 1976.

Gwynn, Frederick L., and Joseph L. Blotner, eds. *Faulkner in the University.* New York: Random House, 1965.

Tape-recorded classroom sessions with Faulkner.

Maugham, W. Somerset. *The Summing Up.* New York: New American Library, 1951.

Roberts, Kenneth. *I Wanted to Write.* New York: Doubleday, 1949.

The Craft of Fiction

Curry, Peggy Simpson. *Creating Fiction from Experience.* Boston: The Writer, 1969.

De Voto, Bernard. *The World of Fiction.* Boston: The Writer, 1962.

Elwood, Maren. *Characters Make Your Story.* Boston: The Writer, 1966.

Fugate, Francis L. *Viewpoint: Key to Fiction Writing.* Boston: The Writer, 1971.

Hersey, John. *Writer's Craft.* New York: Alfred Knopf, 1974.

Koontz, Dean R. *Writing Popular Fiction.* Cincinnati: Writer's Digest, 1972.

Lubbock, Percy. *The Craft of Fiction.* New York: Viking, 1957.

Meredith, Scott. *Writing to Sell.* 2nd revised edition. New York: Harper and Row, 1974.

188 Owen, Jean Z. *Professional Fiction Writing.* Boston: The Writer, 1968.

Polti, Georges. *The Thirty-six Dramatic situations.* Boston: The Writer, 1942.

This is one of the very first books on the basic plots or situations and is still valuable.

Rockwell, F. A. *Modern Fiction Techniques.* Boston: The Writer, 1969.

Shaw, Harry. *Writing and Rewriting.* New York: Harper and Row, 1973.

Somerlott, Robert. *The Writing of Modern Fiction.* Boston: The Writer, 1971.

Wharton, Edith. *Writing of Fiction.* New York: Octagon Press, 1967.

Whitney, Phyllis A. *Writing Juvenile Fiction.* Boston: The Writer, 1962.

Woodford, Jack. *Writing and Selling.* New York: Perma Giants, 1949.
Old and difficult to get hold of today—but worth it if you can. Still the classic in this field because of—not despite—its biting irreverence concerning the world of publishing.

Writing the Novel

Burack, A. S. *Techniques of Novel Writing.* Boston: The Writer, 1968.
Dostoevsky, Fyodor. *The Notebooks for Crime and Punishment,* ed. Edward Wasiolek. Chicago: University of Chicago Press, 1967.
Other Dostoevsky notebooks are also available.
Forster, E. M. *Aspects of the Novel.* New York: Harcourt Brace Jovanovich, 1947.
Frankau, Pamela. *Pen to Paper: A Novelist's Notebook.* New York: Doubleday, 1962.
Hale, Nancy *The Realities of Fiction.* Boston: Little, Brown, 1962.
James, Henry. *The Art of the Novel.* New York: Scribner's, 1934.
Macauley, Robie & George Lanning. *Technique in Fiction.* New York: Harper and Row, 1964.
Mann, Thomas. *The Story of a Novel.* New York: Alfred Knopf, 1961.
This is Mann's account of what he went through writing *Doctor Faustus.*
Meredith, Robert C. & John D. Fitzgerald. *Structuring Your Novel.* New York: Barnes & Noble, 1972.
O'Hara, Mary. *Novel in the Making.* New York: David McKay, 1954.
Winfield, Dick. *One Way to Write Your Novel.* Cincinnati: Writer's Digest, 1969.
Wolf, Thomas. *The Story of a Novel.* New York: Scribner's 1936.

Writing the Short Story

Bates, H. E. *The Modern Short Story.* Boston: The Writer, 1967.
O'Connor, Frank. *The Lonely Voice: A Study of the Short Story.* Cleveland: World Publishing, 1963.

index